Eavesdropping on Paul

Eavesdropping on Paul

Reading Others' Biblical Mail

MARK G. BOYER

St. Romans
P 1 Corinthians
  2 Corinthians
A Galatians
U Philippians
l 1 Thessalonians
  Philemon

RESOURCE *Publications* · Eugene, Oregon

EAVESDROPPING ON PAUL
Reading Others' Biblical Mail

Resource Publications
An Imprint of Wipf and Stock Publishers
199 W. 8th Ave., Suite 3
Eugene, OR 97401

www.wipfandstock.com

PAPERBACK ISBN: 979-8-3852-4725-7
HARDCOVER ISBN: 979-8-3852-4726-4
EBOOK ISBN: 979-8-3852-4727-1

VERSION NUMBER 050725

Dedicated to

All Pauline scholars,

Who made this book possible

. . . Paul [is] a theological minefield or, better, all mine and no field—to his credit then and his challenge still.

—John Dominic Crossan

Contents

Abbreviations

BIBLES

NRSV = The Access Bible: New Revised Standard Version

NRSVue = New Revised Standard Version Updated Edition

TM = The Message: Catholic/Ecumenical Edition

CB (NT) = Christian Bible (New Testament)

Col = Letter to the Colossians

1 Cor = First Letter of Paul to the Corinthians

2 Cor = Second Letter of Paul to the Corinthians

Eph = Letter to the Ephesians

Gal = Letter of Paul to the Galatians

Luke = Luke's Gospel

Mark = Mark's Gospel

Matt = Matthew's Gospel

2 Pet = Second Letter of Peter

Phil = Letter of Paul to the Philippians

Phlm = Letter of Paul to Phileomn

Rev = Revelation

Rom = Letter of Paul to the Romans

1 Thess = First Letter of Paul to the Thessalonians

2 Thess = Second Letter to the Thessalonians

CE = Common Era (same as AD = *Anno Domini*, in the year of the Lord)

HB (OT) = Hebrew Bible (Old Testament)

Dan = Daniel

Deut = Deuteronomy

Exod = Exodus

Gen = Genesis

Hab = Habakkuk

Hos = Hosea

Isa = Isaiah

Jer = Jeremiah

Ps = Psalm

PUNCTUATION USAGE

/ = indicates where one line of poetic text ends and another begins

(biblical notation) = see the specific biblical verse(s) in parentheses for more information

– = range of verses following a colon (8:3–4)

— = range of verses from a verse in one chapter to a verse in another chapter (8:3—9:4)

a, b, c = designates first (a), second (b), third (c), etc. sentence in a verse of Scripture or a line of poetic text

St. Romans
P 1 Corinthians
   2 Corinthians
A Galatians
U Philippians
1 1 Thessalonians
   Philemon

Introduction

EVERY YEAR MULTIPLE PUBLISHERS and multiple biblical scholars present multiple books about Christian Bible (New Testament) Paul. Every biblical scholar attempts to create order out of chaos when it comes to Paul. As John Dominic Cross states (in the epigram): "Paul [is] a theological minefield, or, better, all mine and no field—to his credit then and his challenge still." If there were only one Paul in the CB (NT), it would not be so difficult to understand him. However, there are three faces (and maybe more) of Paul found in the Bible. In biblical book order, there is the Acts-of-the-Apostles Paul; this Paul is generated by the same author—whoever he was—known as the author of Luke's Gospel. Second, there is genuine Paul, the author of seven letters to the Romans, First and Second Corinthians, Galatians, Philippians, First Thessalonians, and Philemon. Third, there are the multiple faces of second-generation Paul; these faces represent believers who updated Paul for their world long after Paul passed from recorded history: Second Thessalonians, Colossians, Ephesians, First and Second Timothy, and Titus. Some Pauline scholars debate the first three letters in this list, but most do not. This book is based on the seven undisputed Pauline letters listed above. This book is not a commentary,

1

but reflections on genuine Pauline theology with meditation/journal questions for developing genuine Pauline understanding and spirituality.

The order of the chapters follows the order of the letters in the Christian Bible (New Testament), not the historical order determined by biblical scholars. In general, the CB (NT) presents the entire body of Paul's letters according to length with the longest (Romans) first and the shortest (Philemon) last. While biblical scholars may differ on the historical order, chronologically most follow this order: Galatians (48 CE), 1 Thessalonians (49–51 CE), 1 Corinthians (53–55 CE), 2 Corinthians (55–56 CE), Romans (57 CE), Philippians (62 CE), and Philemon (62 CE). The order of the chapters in this book follows the order of the seven genuine letters of Paul in the Christian Bible (New Testament), not the historical order determined by biblical scholars above. This author recommends reading the whole letter from the Bible before reading the individual selections presented in this book. When confronting difficult material, continue reading to get the general picture of what (Saul) Paul is writing about.

The seven chapters in this book reflect upon the theological highlights in a genuine Pauline letter; in other words, this is not a commentary, and it is not exhaustive. Household codes—first-century (then current) behavior, according to Paul—are ignored, because we no longer live in the first century common era. While this author tries not to duplicate genuine Pauline, theological ideas, it is inevitable that he does, because Paul phrases them differently in different letters. The reader must keep in mind that a letter was written to a specific group of people at a particular time in history with a specific cultural background: Jews and Gentiles. Modern people are not Romans, Corinthians, Galatians, Philippians, nor Thessalonians! They do not live in the first century common era, nor do they divide themselves into categories of Jews (circumcised) and Gentiles (uncircumcised).

Modern readers of CB (NT) Paul must keep in mind that a letter was written to a specific group of people (Romans, Galatians, Thessalonians) at a particular time in history (first century CE) with a specific cultural background: Jews and Gentiles. Modern readers are not Romans, Corinthians, or Philippians, nor can they read the Greek in which the letters were originally written; they need English translations. They do not live in the first century CE world, nor do they consciously divide themselves into only groups of Jews and Gentiles. At the time Paul was writing, what is now known as the Christian Bible (New Testament) did not yet exist. And, hypothetically it is doubtful that Paul thought he was writing Christian Bible (New Testament) letters!

In the United States of America—as well as in some other countries—people think that the way to change people is by creating laws. Thus, to stop excessive speed on highways, legislatures write a law and post speed-zone signs, but those actions do not change human behavior. A change in behavior occurs because a change has first taken place in the mind caused by hearing a lecture on the dangers of speeding, watching a podcast showing what happens when a speeder plows into another vehicle, or looking at photographs of speeders who did not survive the accident in which they were involved and may have caused.

Saul, a Jew, became Paul, after an eye-opening experience that caused a change in his thinking. As a Torah-abiding Pharisee, in light of the experience he named Jesus Anointed, he had to deal with this question: If righteousness (salvation) could be earned by keeping all 613 precepts of Torah, then what did Jesus do? The answer at which Paul arrived was that God made all people righteous—not by their Torah observance but by their faith that Jesus died, was buried, and raised from the dead by God. In Paul's view, Torah was only for a time, and a person could not earn righteousness anyway. This meant that God had opened the door not only to Jews—to be set free from Torah—but to Gentiles, who did not observe Torah. The change in mind that Paul preached would, hopefully, lead to a change in behavior for both Jews and Gentiles (Greeks). When Paul writes about behavior, it is in the light of faith. In other words, once God made people righteous, they respond with behavior that illustrates faith in Jesus Anointed. Thus, Pauline "Christianity" calls people to do what is the right thing to do (to behave according to faith) because it is the right thing to do. They are to imitate God, who did the right thing in making people righteous (saving them) because it was the right thing for him to do!

Paul faced Judaizers—those who couldn't change their minds nor behavior. They were stuck in Torah observance, especially the practice of circumcision. For Paul, it didn't matter, because it was a work that could not earn righteousness. What is (was) righteousness is always ambiguous; it depends on the situation, the time, the place, and the culture. Paul situated every theological idea in the community, calling it the body of Christ. Modern people live in an individualized theological bubble today. It is not about how God justifies (saves) all, but about how one gets to heaven—earns his or her place there! Thus, to read genuine Pauline letters is to enter a world view foreign to many (most?) people.

EAVESDROPPING ON PAUL: READING OTHERS' BIBLICAL MAIL

Eavesdropping on Paul

Eavesdropping usually refers to listening to a private conversation without the speakers being aware of it. All who read Paul's letters are eavesdroppers! Paul did not write a letter to those living in St. Louis, Missouri. He wrote to those living in Rome, Corinth, Galatia, Philippi, Thessaloniki, and those meeting in Philemon's house in what we today call the first century CE. Thus, when reading Paul's letters, readers are eavesdropping on Paul's correspondence. It is like finding your grandfather's love letters to your grandmother and reading them; you are eavesdropping, even if both of them are dead! Furthermore, you are reading them without context: Were they written while your grandfather was a soldier in the U.S., in Germany, or in England? How old was he? Was he in a branch of the armed forces? Such questions, and more, must be answered in order to understand the letters. But you are still eavesdropping!

Reading Other's Biblical Mail

Not a single letter in the stack of Pauline letters is addressed to you. You are reading other's biblical mail. It is an invasion of privacy! Of course that does not keep people from doing it. Reading others' biblical mail requires knowledge of who the original addressee was, where he or she lived, when he or she lived, his or her culture, and the same about the sender of the letter. Without such information, conclusions may be reached that do not cohere or make much sense.

This is the case quite often with Paul's letters. Some people pick small parts from his correspondence that enhance their own or their church's theology and ignore the rest of the letter. Thus, Paul is often made to say things he didn't write! This is best seen especially in second generation Pauline letters. For example, in no genuine Pauline letter is the Anointed (Christ) named as head of the church. In genuine Pauline thought, all believers are equal members living in love. However, in second generation letters, the Anointed is named head of the church, his body. The change reflects a time later than Paul, when his small groups of believers have become an institution with a governing hierarchy.

EXERCISES

Each chapter of this book contains selections from one of Paul's genuine letters. Each exercise has a title that alerts the reader to the subject of the exercise. The title is followed by a quotation (Scripture) from the letter under investigation, followed by a Reflection, which explains the Scripture in its context and gives insights concerning its meaning to its intended readers. A Meditation/Journal question follows; it asks the reader to apply the information in the Reflection to his or her life, an act of spirituality. Finally, a Psalm Response presents a few verses of a psalm that echo an idea, word, or perspective uncovered in the Reflection and meant to bring the exercise to a close.

The writer's goal is to urge familiarity with the totality of Pauline thought spread through the seven authentic letters of Paul and to mine them for both what the Apostle says in them, even if it may contradict promulgated theological thought today.

BIBLE NOTES

The Bible is divided into two parts: The Hebrew Bible (Old Testament) and the Christian Bible (New Testament). The Hebrew Bible consists of thirty-nine named books accepted by Jews and Protestants as Holy Scripture. The Old Testament also contains those thirty-nine books plus seven to fifteen more named books or parts of books called the Apocrypha or the Deuterocanonical Books; the Old Testament is accepted by Catholics and several other Christian denominations as Holy Scripture. The Christian Bible, consisting of twenty-seven named books, is also called the New Testament; it is accepted by Christians as Holy Scripture. Thus, in this work:

—**Hebrew Bible (Old Testament)**, abbreviated **HB (OT)**, indicates that a book is found both in the Hebrew Bible and the Old Testament;

—and **Christian Bible (New Testament)**, abbreviated **CB (NT)**, indicates that a book is found only in the Christian Bible or New Testament.

In notating biblical texts, the first number refers to the chapter in the book, and the second number (following the colon) refers to the verse within the chapter. Thus, HB (OT) Isa 7:11 means that the quotation comes from Isaiah, chapter 7, verse 11. CB (NT) Rom 6:2 means that the quotation comes from Paul's Letter to the Romans, chapter 6, verse 2. When more than one sentence appears in a verse, the letters a, b, c, etc. indicate the sentence being referenced in the verse. Thus, HB (OT) 2 Kgs 1:6a means that the quotation comes from the Second Book of Kings, chapter 1, verse 6, sentence 1. Also, poetry, such as the Psalms and sections of Judith, Proverbs, Isaiah, and others may be noted using the letters a, b, c, etc. to indicate the lines being used. Thus, Ps 16:4a refers to the first line of verse 4 of Psalm 16; there are two more lines of verse 4: b and c.

In the HB (OT), the reader often sees LORD (note all capital letters). Because God's name (Yahweh or YHWH, referred to as the Tetragrammaton) is not to be pronounced, the name Adonai (meaning *Lord*) is substituted for Yahweh when a biblical text is read. When a biblical text is translated and printed, LORD (Gen 2:4) is used to alert the reader to what the text actually states: Yahweh. Furthermore, when the biblical author writes Lord Yahweh, printers present Lord GOD (note all capital letters for GOD; Gen 15:2) to avoid the printed ambiguity of LORD LORD. The Psalms in *The Message*, substitutes GOD (note all capital letters) for Yahweh. When the reference is to Jesus, the word printed is Lord (note capital L and lower-case letters; Luke 11:1).

Also, most Bible editors do not translate the Greek word *Christos*; they merely transliterate it into *Christ*. Throughout this book, I refer to Jesus Anointed or Anointed Jesus; *anointed* is the English translation of the Greek *Christos*. In his letters, Paul uses the descriptive word *anointed* for Jesus to indicate that he was chosen (anointed) by God for a specific mission.

In this book, *cf* (meaning *confer*) has not been used. Biblical notations placed in parentheses indicate where the reference can be found in the Bible. For example, the Second Book of Samuel records King David writing a song (2 Sam 22:1–51). The notation in parentheses is given to the reader, who may wish to look up the full reference in his or her Bible. In some instances, a few notations appear in parentheses; again, the reader may wish to see the references in their contexts.

Bibles

Most Bible readers are not aware that there is no such thing as the original Bible! The fact is: There are Bibles. First, there is the Jewish Bible, often called the Hebrew Bible; its books were collected and completed between 70 and 90 CE based on the Jerusalem canon (collection) in this order: Torah (Genesis, Exodus, Leviticus,

Numbers, Deuteronomy), Prophets (Isaiah, Jeremiah, Ezekiel, etc.), and Writings (Job, Psalms, Proverbs, etc.). It is important to note the arrangement of the collected books. Second, there is—for want of a better name—the Christian Hebrew Bible, completed in the fourth century CE, but not defined until after the Reformation. It consists of Torah, Writings, and Prophets. It is important to note the (re)ordering of the collected books. Christianity took the Jewish (Hebrew) Bible and rearranged the order of its books! Then, Christianity named it the Old Testament.

The Jerusalem canon, obviously, is the collection of biblical books used in Jerusalem and its environs. A large community of Jews, however, lived in Alexandria, Egypt. To the Jerusalem canon (books in Hebrew and Aramaic) they added books in Greek, the language they spoke; this collection is the Alexandrine canon. They also translated the Jerusalem canon's books from Hebrew and Aramaic into Greek. That translation, containing books and parts of books not in the Jerusalem canon, is called the Septuagint (abbreviated LXX). Later, the Septuagint was translated into Latin; it is known as the Vulgate. Every time a book of the Bible is translated, it picks up something and it loses something; that is because there is no such thing as literary equivalence.

Thus, we have (1) the Hebrew Bible—the Jewish Bible, (2) the Hebrew Bible (Old Testament)—the rearranged books of the Hebrew Bible, and (3) the Christian Bible—twenty-seven books originally written in Greek. The Protestant Bible contains only the books in the Jerusalem canon, but rearranged into the Old Testament, plus the Christian Bible books; the Catholic Bible contains the books in the Alexandrine collection plus the Christian Bible books.

The extra books or parts of books found in the Catholic Bible (and coming from the Alexandrine collection of the Jewish Bible), but not found in a Protestant Bible, are collectively referred to as the Apocrypha or Deuterocanonical Books. They include Tobit, Judith, additions to Esther, Wisdom of Solomon, Sirach (Ecclesiasticus), Baruch, Letter of Jeremiah, Prayer of Azariah (addition to Daniel), Susanna (addition to Daniel), Bel and the Dragon (addition to Daniel), 1 Maccabees, 2 Maccabees, 1 Esdras, Prayer of Manasseh, Psalm 151, 3 Maccabees, 2 Esdras, and 4 Maccabees. Not every Christian group, such as Catholics, accepts all the books in the Apocrypha as Scripture; for example, out of the four books of Maccabees, Catholics accept only 1 and 2 Maccabees. In Catholic Bibles, the additional books are placed with similar books. Thus, First and Second Maccabees are inserted with the historical books; the books of Wisdom and Sirach are found in the wisdom literature section.

Thus, there is no single or original Bible; there are many Bibles; it depends on what books a specific denomination or group (Jews, Christians) accepts as Scripture. The Bible that contains any book that any group accepts as Scripture is *The Access Bible* (updated edition): *New Revised Standard Version with the Apocrypha,* (NRSV) general editors Gail R. O'Day and David Petersen, published in New York by Oxford University Press in 1999 and updated in 2011.

In 2022, Zondervan published the New Revised Standard Version Updated Edition (NRSVue) to ensure the currency and integrity of the NRSVue as the most up-to-date and reliable Bible for use and study in the English language. The NRSVue contains approximately 12,000 substantive edits and 20,000 total changes made to the NRSV.

In this book in general, the NRSVue is used for the Scriptures, while Eugene M. Peterson's and William Griffin's The Message is used for the Psalm Responses.

Thus, a Bible reader should keep in mind the following: In a Christian Bible, The Old Testament consists of the rearranged books found in the Hebrew (Jewish) Bible. Roman Catholics and some others add some books and parts of books to that Old Testament because they were found in the Alexandrine collection. In general, Protestants do not add books to the Old Testament; they follow the Jerusalem collection of books, but rearrange them as noted above. Almost all Christians accept the twenty-seven books of the New Testament; there are a few groups that reject one or another of the books in the collection.

Before the formation of the Christian Bible (New Testament) Paul's Letters were gathered and circulated as a collection separate from the other books that became the New Testament. A point often overlooked by modern readers is the fact that they are not the intended readers of Pauline texts. Every Pauline letter was written to a specific group of people at a specific time in history. Thus, Paul did not write to people living in the United States; he wrote in Greek to people living in Rome, Corinth, and Thessalonica. Modern readers are reading an English translation (and interpretation) with Roman-Greco cultural presuppositions underlying the text.

Furthermore, letters were not first intended to be read privately as is done today. They were meant to be heard in a group. The very low rate of literacy in the first century would have never dictated many copies of texts since most people could not read, and their standard practice was to listen to another read the letters to them. The letters of Paul are older than the gospels. As already noted above, biblical scholars divide the letters of Paul into the authentic letters—those written by Paul (Romans, Galatians, Philippians, etc.)—and those written by someone else in Paul's name—second generation Pauline letters (Ephesians, Colossians, Titus, etc.). The latter group of letters usually develop Pauline thought for a new generation of Christians. The reader of letters needs to keep in mind that the letter was not addressed to him or her; it was addressed to a specific group of believers in the mid- to late-first century CE. In addition to the Pauline body of letters, there are other letters that were gathered and placed in the CB (NT) canon (collection), such as James, 1 and 2 Peter, Jude, etc. These anonymous letters were written in the name of an apostle to give them authority in the Christian communities to which they were addressed.

A FEW BOOKS ON PAUL

Below are listed a few books on Pauline thought for readers who want to locate original Paul in his own context.

Crossan, John Dominic. *Paul the Pharisee: A Vision Beyond the Violence of Civilization*. Salem, OR: Polebridge, 2024.

Hartin, Patrick J. *A Window into the Spirituality of Paul.* Collegeville, MN: Liturgical, 2015.

Hoover, Roy W. *The Prospect of a New Humanity: The Origin of Paul's Gospel and a New Reading of its Meaning.* Salem, OR: Polebridge, 2024.

Scott, Bernard Brandon. *The Real Paul: Recovering His Radical Challenge.* Salem, OR: Polebridge, 2015.

Thiessen, Matthew. *A Jewish Paul: The Messiah's Herald to the Gentiles.* Grand Rapids, MI: Baker Academic, 2023.

St. Romans
P 1 Corinthians
   2 Corinthians
A Galatians
U Philippians
1 1 Thessalonians
   Philemon

1

Romans

SERVANT

Scripture: "Paul, a servant of Christ Jesus . . . ." (Rom 1:1, NRSVue)
Reflection: In both his Letter to the Romans and his Letter to the Philippians (1:1), Paul refers to himself as a servant. Some English translations choose bond-servant or slave. While slave is the more accurate translation, it can carry negative connotations. As a slave, Paul writes on behalf of his master. In other words, he is an agent of Anointed Jesus, and he considers himself to be at the bottom of the social ladder, as a slave. Most English translations do not translate Christ, a Greek word meaning anointed. The Anointed Jesus or Jesus Anointed refers to one set apart and the authority the one set apart enjoys. Thus, Paul considers himself a slave of the one who was set apart by God for a specific mission.

Meditation/Journal: Of whom are you a slave (servant)? Explain.

Psalm Response: ". . . [T]hose who want / the best for me, [GOD,] / Let them have the last word—a glad shout!— / and say, over and over and over, / 'GOD is great—everything works / together for good for his servant.' / I'll tell the world how great and good you are, / I'll shout Hallelujah all day, every day." (Ps 35:27–28, TM)

APOSTLE

Scripture: "Paul, . . . , called to be an apostle . . . ." (Rom 1:1, NRSVue)

Reflection: Paul considers himself called by God to be an apostle. The Greek word for apostle means someone sent on behalf of someone else; he is an envoy. In his Letter to the Galatians, he explains that he has been sent "through Jesus Christ and God the Father, who raised him from the dead" (Gal 1:1, NRSVue). Paul discloses that his office as an apostle rests on divine election. He has been chosen and sent by Anointed Jesus and the God-Father, who demonstrated power by raising Jesus from the dead. Later in the Letter to the Romans, Paul states that he is an "apostle to the gentiles" (Rom 11:13, NRSVue). Also, he names himself "a minister of Christ Jesus to the gentiles" (Rom 15:16, NRSVue). Gentiles (sometimes called Greeks) are those who are not Jews.

Meditation/Journal: To what has Anointed Jesus and God called you?

Psalm Response: "I love GOD because he listened to me, / listened as I begged for mercy. / He listened so intently / as I laid out my case before him. / Death stared me in the face, / hell was hard on my heels. / Up against it, I didn't know which way to turn; / then I called out to GOD for help: / 'Please, GOD!' I cried out. / 'Save my life!' / God is gracious—it is he who makes things right, / our most compassionate God." (Ps 116:1–5, TM)

SET APART

Scripture: "Paul, . . . set apart for the gospel of God . . . ." (Rom 1:1, NRSVue)

Reflection: In his letter to the Galatians, Paul states that God set him apart before he was born (Gal 1:15). The basic meaning of set apart is to separate from all else. Paul considers himself set apart by God and sent to Gentiles with the gospel of God. The gospel of God is the good news that God raised Jesus from the dead. Paul declares that God revealed his Son to him so that he could proclaim him to the Gentiles (Gal 1:15). The content of God's gospel is noted in Paul's First Letter to the Corinthians: The Anointed died for sins, he was buried, and he was raised; he appeared to the twelve, many others, and to Paul (1 Cor 15:1–8). Paul was entrusted with the gospel for the uncircumcised (Gentiles) (Gal 2:7). God worked through him by setting him apart and sending him to the Gentiles to preach God's good news to them (Gal 2:8).

Journal/Meditation: For what has God set you apart? Explain.

Psalm Response: "Look at this; look / Who got picked by GOD! / He listens the split second I call to him. / Complain if you must, but don't lash out. / Keep your mouth shut, and let your heart do the talking. / I have God's more-than-enough, / More joy in one ordinary day . . . . (Ps 4:3–4, 6b–7, TM)

PROMISED BEFOREHAND

Scripture: "Paul, . . . set apart for the gospel of God, which he promised beforehand through his prophets in the holy scriptures . . . ." (Rom 1:1–2, NRSVue)

Reflection: The good news (gospel) that Paul proclaims had been promised by God before Paul's time by the prophets in the Hebrew Bible (Old Testament). The God who acted in the past, as recorded in the Hebrew Bible (Old Testament) has acted again in Anointed Jesus. Thus, as far as Paul is concerned there is a divine continuity between the past and the present. There is one God of both Jews and Gentiles. Paul is explicit about this point later in the letter. "[God has made] known the riches of his glory for the objects of mercy, which he has prepared beforehand for glory—including us whom he has called, not from the Jews only but also from the gentiles" (Rom 9:23–24). Again, at the end of the letter, he writes about ". . . God who is able to strengthen . . . according to [his] gospel and the proclamation of Jesus Christ, according to the revelation of the mystery that was kept secret for long ages but is now disclosed and through the prophetic writings is made known to all the gentiles . . ." (Rom 16:25–26). In other words, Paul states that God has been at work for ages, getting ready to disclose the next step of revelation: Jesus Anointed.

Journal/Meditation: What are the five most important steps of divine revelation that have occurred in your life?

Psalm Response: "He's GOD, our God, / in charge of the whole earth. / And he remembers, remembers his Covenant— / for a thousand generation he's been as good as his word. / He permitted no one to abuse [Israel]. / He told kings to keep their hands off; / 'Don't you dare lay a hand on my anointed, / don't hurt a hair on the heads of my prophets.'" (Ps 105:7–8, 14–15, TM)

FLESH AND SPIRIT

Scripture: "Paul, . . . set apart for the gospel of God, . . . the gospel concerning his Son, who was descended from David according to the flesh and was declared to be Son of God with power according to the spirit of holiness by resurrection from the dead, Jesus Christ our Lord . . . ." (Rom 1:1–4, NRSVue)

Reflection: Adapting what many biblical scholars think is a Jewish Christianity primitive creed, Paul conceded that God's Son is descended from the seed of David in terms of flesh, but he was appointed, designated, installed, and enthroned as Son of God in terms of his resurrection. This understanding came to be known as adoptionist Christology. As a primitive Palestinian Christology, adoptionism also appears in the scene in Mark's Gospel depicting Jesus of Nazareth's appearance from Galilee, John the Baptist's baptism of him, and the voice from heaven claiming (adopting)

15

Jesus as his Son (Mark 1:9–11). The primitive flesh-spirit dualism in Greek thought reflects a damnation-salvation dualism. Paul trumps Jesus' fleshly Davidic descent with the Anointed's power of the spirit of holiness by resurrection. Being of the flesh meant that Jesus was bound to the material world; being Anointed meant that he belonged to the sphere of the spirit, a superior world of divine power. In Paul's Letter to the Romans, the gospel about Jesus Anointed is about the power of God for salvation, which resides not in Davidic descent, but in the direct divine appointment of the Anointed Jesus as Son of God with power.

Meditation/Journal: Where do you find flesh-spirit dualism today? Which is dominant?

Psalm Response: "Why the big noise, nations? / Why the mean plots, peoples? / Earth-leaders push for position, / Demagogues and delegates meet for summit talks. / The God-deniers, the Messiah-defiers: / 'Let's get free of God! / Cast loose from Messiah!' / Let me tell you what GOD said . . . . / He said, 'You're my son, / And today is your birthday. / What do you want? Name it: / Nations as a present? Continents as a prize? / You can command them all to dance for you, / Or throw them out with tomorrow's trash.'" (Ps 2:1–3, 7–9, TM)

OBEDIENCE OF FAITH

Scripture: ". . . [T]hrough [Jesus Christ our Lord] we have received grace and apostleship to bring about the obedience of faith among all the gentiles for the sake of his name . . . ." (Rom 1:5, NRSVue)

Reflection: Paul declares that he has received grace through the resurrection of Jesus Anointed. Grace is a gift or favor from God given openly and freely. For Paul, grace is access to God; it is the act of God sharing himself with people without having met any qualifications. Grace overcomes human deficiencies, as Paul makes clear in his Letter to the Galatians. He states, ". . . [T]he one who had set me apart before I was born . . . called me through his grace [and] was pleased to reveal his Son to me" (Gal 1:15–16, NRSVue). Paul links grace and apostleship, being sent to the Gentiles to bring about the obedience of faith, a phrase found here and only one time later in Romans (16:26). Obedience of faith means Gentiles' acceptance of the message of salvation. After hearing Paul's message, Gentiles freely respond to God's gift of grace. Their response is for the sake of Jesus Anointed's name, which is the foundation and theme of Pauline proclamation (Rom 15:20–21).

Meditation/Journal: What specific grace have you received from God? What element of apostleship was in it? What obedience of faith resulted from your acceptance of it?

Psalm Response: "My heart bursts its banks, / spilling beauty and goodness. / I pour it out in a poem to the king, / shaping the river into words: / 'You're the handsomest of men; / every word from your lips is sheer grace, / and God has blessed you, blessed you so much. / Your throne is God's throne, / ever and always . . . . / And that is why God, your very own God, / poured fragrant oil on your head, / Marking you out as king / from among your dear companions.'" (Ps 45:1–2, 6a, 7b, TM)

GRACE AND PEACE

Scripture: "Grace to you and peace from God our Father and the Lord Jesus Christ." (Rom 1:7b, NRSVue)

Reflection: The above greeting closes the first section of Paul's Letter to the Romans. It appears in other genuine Pauline letters (1 Cor 1:3; 2 Cor 1:2; Gal 1:3; Phil 1:2; 1 Thess 1:1; and Phlm 3). It is an adaptation of a Jewish greeting about mercy and peace. For Paul, grace is the essence of what the Anointed provides (Gal 2:21; 1 Cor 1:4; 2 Cor 6:1): unmerited access to God for those who do not deserve it! Peace, without enemies or wild beasts and with prosperity and contentment given by the LORD (Yahweh), carries a distinctive dimension of reconciliation with God. As the Pauline greeting makes clear, the power to grant the content of the blessing—grace and peace—derives not from the person offering it—Paul—but from the source of every blessing—God our Father and the Lord Jesus Anointed.

Meditation/Journal: What grace and peace have you received from God the Father and the Lord Jesus Christ? Explain.

Psalm Response: "Bravo, GOD, bravo! / Gods and all angels shout, 'Encore!' / In awe before the glory, / in awe before God's visible power. / Stand at attention! / Dress your best to honor him! / Above the floodwaters is GOD's throne / from which his power flows, / from which he rules the world. / GOD makes his people strong. / GOD gives his people peace." (Ps 29:1-2, 10-11, TM)

PRAYER

Scripture: "For God, whom I serve with my spirit by announcing the gospel of his Son, is my witness that without ceasing I remember you [Romans] always in my prayers." (Rom 1:9, NRSVue)

Reflection: In the verse above, Paul establishes a formulation of God as his witness, a formula found frequently in his letters (2 Cor 1:23; Phil 1:8; 1 Thess 2:5). Above, he uses the formula to attest to the truthfulness of his claim to be bound in prayer to the Roman believers; in other words, he uses the witness of God to confirm that he is telling the truth that he includes them within the circle of his concern as the apostle to the Gentiles (Rom 15:16). Paul serves God in his spirit, and Paul's spirit is connected to God's Spirit, and that is how he announces the gospel of God's Son, Jesus Anointed. For Paul, genuine prayer comes from God's Spirit (Rom 8:26). Thus, Paul's service of the gospel of God's Son is derived from God's Spirit connected to Paul's spirit. That is why he can write that he prays ceaselessly or constantly (1 Thess 1:2, 2:13, 5:17). Prayer is a state of mind for the apostle, a fact to which God can bear witness.

Meditation/Journal: In what specific ways do you experience the prayers of others? In what specific ways do you experience your spirit being connected to God's Spirit?

Psalm Response: "Listen while I build my case, GOD, / the most honest prayer you'll ever hear. / Show the world I'm innocent— / in your heart you know I am. / Go ahead, examine me from inside out, / surprise me in the middle of the night— / You'll find I'm just what I say I am. / My words don't run loose. / I call to you, God, because I'm sure of an answer. / So—answer! Bend your ear! Listen sharp!" (Ps 17:1–3, 6, TM)

RIGHTEOUSNESS

Scripture: ". . . I am not ashamed of the gospel; it is God's saving power for everyone who believes, for the Jew first and also for the Greek. For in it the righteousness of God is revealed through faith for faith, as it is written, 'The one who is righteous will live by faith.'" (Rom 1:16–17, NRSVue)

Reflection: The above two verses from Paul's Letter to the Romans is the thesis of the letter and its theme: the gospel. Paul's gospel concerns the righteousness of God revealed in the event of Jesus Anointed that is being conveyed by Paul, who is not ashamed of the proclamation about the crucified and raised Anointed. Most people of Paul's day would have been ashamed that the redeemer died on a cross, demeaning God. In his First Letter to the Corinthians, Paul states this clearly: ". . . [W]e proclaim Christ crucified, a stumbling block to Jews and foolishness to gentiles" (1 Cor 1:23). Paul's gospel is revolutionary and paradoxical. The shameful gospel that would not take root, the power of God, is a revelation of God; it is the means of restoring righteous control over disobedient creation. The divine power emanating from the gospel results in salvation. For Paul that divine power is manifest in the powerless communities of faith established by the gospel, so that those groups who place their faith in it will be set right. The triumph of divine righteousness through the gospel of the Anointed crucified and raised turns upside down the cultural system of Paul's day and time. God's power for salvation transforms every group that responds in faith to the gospel concerning the Anointed's crucifixion and resurrection. Whereas the concept of righteousness had been associated with loyalty to the covenant, now, according to Paul, it is the act by which God brings both Jews and Gentiles (Greeks) into right relationship with God. As the gospel spreads, divine righteousness is achieved and salvation is established in faith communities where righteous relationships are maintained. Wholeness is restored on a corporate level, and, consequently, on an individual level. Thus, divine righteousness revealed in the gospel as the power of God ushering in a time of salvation progresses from one transformed community of faith to another transformed community of faith. By altering the verse he found in the prophet Habakkuk (2:4), Paul explains that faith refers to acceptance of his gospel. Paul's preaching of the gospel establishes communities of faith in which God restores salvation for those who believe in the crucified and raised Anointed One.

Meditation/Journal: In what specific ways have you experienced God's righteousness (saving power)?

Psalm Response: "In you, O LORD, I seek refuge; / do not let me ever be put to shame; / in your righteousness deliver me. / Into your hand I commit my spirit; / you have redeemed me, O LORD, faithful God. / Let your face shine upon your servant; / save me in your steadfast love. / Do not let me be put to shame, O LORD, / for I call on you . . . ." (Ps 31: 1, 5, 16–17a, NRSV)

CIRCUMCISION

Scripture: ". . . [A] person is not a Jew who is one outwardly, nor is circumcision something external and physical. Rather, a person is a Jew who is one inwardly, and circumcision is a matter of the heart, by the Spirit, not the written code. Such a person receives praise not from humans but from God." (Rom 2:28–29, NRSVue)

Reflection: Circumcision, literally meaning *to cut around*, is the physical removal of the foreskin from the male penis. In the Hebrew Bible (Old Testament), circumcision is the sign of entering into the covenant God made with Abraham (Gen 17:1–14). Paul saw that the outward—in the flesh—sign of circumcision did not indicate that the man kept the Torah; in fact, he often witnessed the opposite. That is why he writes that circumcision is not the sole measurement of being a Jew. The real measurement of being Jewish is found within a person; circumcision is a matter of one's whole being (heart) by the Spirit. Since it is a matter of the heart, both

Jews and Gentiles can approach God with a heart transformed by the Spirit. This means that those who keep Torah are not necessarily Jewish; it also means that those who are called Gentiles can be keepers of Torah without being Jewish (circumcised). It is not the letter of Torah that matters, but it is the Spirit of Torah that matters. Those who receive the gift of a circumcised heart rely on God's praises alone. With a few strokes of his pen Paul has reduced both Jews and Gentiles to one common denominator: both need to be made righteous and saved by God.

Meditation/Journal: In what specific ways has your heart been transformed by the Spirit? What practical application can you make of Paul's words (argument) today?

Psalm Response: "I'm thanking you, GOD, from a full heart, / I'm writing the book on your wonders. / I'm whistling, laughing, and jumping for joy; / I'm singing your song, High God. / GOD holds the high center, / he sees and sets the world's mess right. / He decides what is right for us earthlings, / gives people their just des[s]erts." (Ps 9:1–2, 7–8, TM)

JUSTIFIED BY GRACE

Scripture: ". . . [N]ow, apart from the law, the righteousness of God has been disclosed and is attested by the Law and the Prophets, the righteousness of God through the faith of Jesus Christ for all who believe. For there is no distinction, since all have sinned and fall short of the glory of God; they are now justified by his grace as a gift, through the redemption that is in Christ Jesus." (Rom 3:21–24, NRSVue)

Reflection: At the time of Paul, the Pharisee, righteousness was achieved by adhering to the 613 laws in Torah. However, Paul states that God's righteousness has been disclosed apart from the law. In his Letter to the Galatians, Paul is even clearer: ". . . [W]e know that a person is justified not by the works of the law but through the faith of Jesus Christ. And we have come to believe in Christ Jesus, so that we might be justified by the faith of Christ and not by doing the works of the law, because no one will be justified by the works of the law." (Gal 2:16, NRSVue). God's righteousness is God's saving activity in the crucified Anointed One that sets the world right. God's power restores the glory of creation with a new creation. According to Paul, divine righteousness became visible in the Christ event, a different method of divine revelation, because the law was not able to place its adherents in a right relationship with God. Jesus Anointed's faith is God's means of offering to all—Jews and Gentiles—righteousness in response to the gospel with faith. Paul declares that all people are sinners and in need of the free gift of grace that justifies. Faith, for Paul, denotes assent to and participation in the gospel of the crucified and raised Anointed One that reveals the righteousness of God and transcends all barriers. Salvation is equally available to all because it is a divine gift that cannot be achieved by human effort (Torah). The offer of grace to all removes all possibility of anyone boasting (Rom 3:27–30).

Meditation/Journal: What are the consequences of Paul's radical inclusivity? Explain.

Psalm Response: "Oh, thank GOD—he's so good! / His love never runs out. / All of you set free by GOD, tell the world! / Tell how he freed you from oppression, / Then rounded you up from all over the place, / from the four winds, from the seven seas. / So thank God for his marvelous love, / for his miracle mercy to the children he loves." (Ps 107:1–3, 8, TM)

BOASTING

Scripture: ". . . [W]hat becomes of boasting? It is excluded. Through what kind of law? That of works? No, rather through the law of faith. For we hold that a person is justified by faith apart from works prescribed by the law. Or is God the God of the Jews only? Is he not the God of gentiles also? Yes, of gentiles also, since God is one and he will justify the circumcised on the ground of faith and the uncircumcised through that same faith. Do we then overthrow the law through this faith? By no means!" (Rom 3:27–31b, NRSVue)

Reflection: In the small communities in Rome, Paul had heard about boasting; some groups of believers were speaking proudly about their accomplishments—they were praising themselves. Because Rome was the capital of the empire, it was the boasting champion of Paul's world; it was filled with monuments and celebrations of achievement. In Paul's schema, salvation by grace alone renders problematic all human boasting. As he usually does, Paul reduces all small communities—both Jewish and Gentile—to the same common denominator: faith. The law of works, following Torah, results in boasting, because a person does the works. The law of faith, derived from Jesus Anointed, excludes boasting. According to Paul, God's activity in Jesus Anointed sets right a fallen world by granting righteousness to all. Being set right with God by God through the Anointed One means that as God chose a people (Hebrews, Israelites, Jews) in the past, through Jesus Anointed he has chosen all people, lavished grace on them, and offered them grace which is salvation. The purpose of the law was to reveal sin (Rom 3:20); "the law was our disciplinarian until Christ came, so that we might be reckoned as righteous by faith" (Rom 3:24, NRSVue). Thus, because grace is a free gift from God, no one can boast; all—Jews (the circumcised) and Gentiles (the uncircumcised)—are justified by faith. In Paul's own words: "For God has done what the law, weakened by the flesh, could not do by sending his own Son in the likeness of sinful flesh and to deal with sin, he condemned sin in the flesh" (Rom 8:3, NRSVue). "Let the one who boasts, boast in the Lord" (1 Cor 1:31, NRSVue).

Meditation/Journal: If a person is justified by faith apart from works prescribed by the law, what is the purpose of circumcision? of the ten commandments? of church doctrines and dogmas?

Psalm Response: "I bless GOD every chance I get; / my lungs expand with his praise. / I live and breathe GOD; / if things aren't going well, hear this and be happy: / Join me in spreading the news; / together let's get the word out. / GOD met me more than halfway, / he freed me from my anxious fears. / Look at him; give him your warmest smile. / Never hide your feelings from him. / Open your mouth and taste, open your eyes and see— / how good GOD is. / Blessed are you who run to him." (Ps 34:1–5, 8, TM)

ABRAHAM

Scripture: "What then are we to say was gained by Abraham, our ancestor according to the flesh? For if Abraham was justified by works, he has something to boast about, but not before God. For what does the scripture say? 'Abraham believed God, and it was reckoned to him as righteousness.' How then was it reckoned to him? Was it before or after he had been circumcised? It was not after but before he was circumcised. He received the sign of circumcision as a seal of the righteousness that he had by faith while he was still uncircumcised. The purpose was to make him the ancestor of all who believe without being circumcised and who thus have righteousness reckoned to them, and likewise the ancestor of the circumcised who are not only circumcised but follow the example of the faith that our ancestor Abraham had before he was circumcised." (Rom 4:1–3, 10–12, NRSVue)

Reflection: The text above from Paul's Letter to the Romans is long, but its entirety is necessary to display what the author thinks he has discovered in the Hebrew Bible (Old Testament) book of Genesis: ". . . [Abram] believed the LORD's promise about having countless descendants] and the LORD reckoned it to him as righteousness" (Gen 15:6, NRSVue). This occurs before Abram is instructed by the LORD to "circumcise the flesh of [his] foreskin, and it shall be sign of the covenant between [the LORD] and him" (Gen 17:11, NRSVue). According to Paul, Abraham had performed no religious work before the LORD declared him righteous. In Paul's view, this makes Abraham the parent of all believers, no matter whether they are circumcised or not. Whoever trusts God's promises is righteous, both Jews and Gentiles. It is not on the basis of works that Abraham is declared righteous, but on the basis of God's mercy which suffices for justification for both Jews and Gentiles. Paul declares that Abraham's circumcision was a seal of the righteous status he had received previously.

Thus, circumcision is a sign of his righteousness through faith. Just as Abraham was accepted as righteous before God (before he was circumcised), uncircumcised Gentiles can be accepted as righteous before God. Abraham is not only the forefather of the Jewish people (the circumcised), but he is also the forefather of the Gentiles (the uncircumcised), who have responded to the message of the unconditional grace of Jesus Anointed. Thus, the focus is not on the primacy of circumcision, but on the primacy of faith, which establishes a unified group identity.

In his Letter to the Galatians, Paul revisits his point about righteousness coming to all people through grace. "Just as Abraham 'believed God, and it was reckoned to him as righteousness,'" writes Paul to the Galatians, "see, those who believe are the descendants of Abraham" (Gal 3:6–7, NRSVue). Then, he adds, ". . . [T]he scripture, foreseeing that God would reckon as righteous the gentiles by faith, declared the gospel beforehand to Abraham saying 'All the gentiles shall be blessed in you.' For this reason, those who believe are blessed with Abraham who believed." (Gal 3:8–9, NRSVue). Paul attributes a unique role to Abraham; he was the only person before Jesus Anointed who knew the gospel and believed in it. Thus, Abraham, who in Judaism is the representative of righteousness through obedience to Torah, is made the representative of people of faith, those who believe in the God who justifies the unrighteous.

Meditation/Journal: Read the Letter of James 2:18–26. What do you discover the difference to be between James and Paul? What are the consequences of your discovery?

Psalm Response: "I waited and waited and waited for GOD. / At last he looked; finally he listened. / He taught me how to sing the latest God-song, / a praise-song to our God. / I've preached you to the whole congregation, / I've kept back nothing, GOD—you know that. / I didn't keep the news of your ways / a secret, didn't keep it to myself. / I told it all, how dependable you are, how thorough. / I didn't hold back pieces of love and truth / For myself alone. I told it all, / let the congregation know the whole story." (Ps 40:1, 3, 9–10, TM)

GOD'S PROMISE

Scripture: ". . . [T]he promise that he would inherit the world did not come to Abraham or to his descendants through the law but through the righteousness of faith. For this reason the promise depends on faith, in order that it may rest on grace, so that it may be guaranteed to all his descendants, not only to the adherents of the law but also to those who share the faith of Abraham (who is the father of all of us, as it is written, 'I have made you the father of many nations'), in the presence of the God in whom he believed, who gives life to the dead and calls into existence the things that do not exist. Hoping against hope, he believed that he would become 'the father of many nations' . . . . He did not weaken in faith . . . . No distrust made him waver concerning the promise of God, but he grew strong in his faith as he gave glory to God, being fully convinced that God was able to do what he had promised. Therefore 'it was reckoned to him as righteousness.' . . . It will be reckoned to us who believe in him who raised Jesus our Lord from the dead, who was handed over for our trespasses and was raised for our justification." (Rom 4:13, 16–23, 25, NRSVue)

Reflection: In Genesis 17:5, after the LORD changes Abram's name to Abraham, the LORD states, "I have made you the ancestor of a multitude of nations." Paul understands that to mean that Abraham would inherit the world, which had already begun—not through the law—through the righteousness of faith. The formula is the path believers can follow to be declared righteous and join the community in acceptance of the gospel of God's righteousness made present in the Anointed. For Paul, faith is best defined as grace, access to God by God granted without any prior conditions; all one needs to do is to accept the offer. This means that the promise to all Abraham's descendants is valid for both Jews and Gentiles. The promise made to Abraham establishes an inclusivity for all people of faith. Abraham is Paul's example of one who continued to believe in God, to hope that God would fulfill the promise; he did not weaken or waver; he refused to give up hope in God's power. The Pauline paradox states that Abraham hoped against hope! God's power to evoke faith, trust, results in Abraham's righteousness; Abraham enjoyed a relationship with God that he did not earn. Paul's understanding of Abraham prepares the way to acknowledge the gospel: Jesus Anointed's death and resurrection opens the way for all—Jews and Gentiles—to receive grace and to be reckoned right before God by God. All are heirs of Abraham's promise; all share Abraham's faith that God gives life to the dead and creates (gives existence to) what did not exist.

Meditation/Journal: How do you define faith? How does your definition of faith compare to Paul's definition? What promise have you received from God?

Psalm Response: "Hallelujah! / Thank GOD! Pray to him by name! / Tell everyone you meet what he has done! / Sing him songs, belt out hymns, / translate his wonders into music! / Honor his holy name with Hallelujahs, / you who seek GOD. Live a happy life! / Keep your eyes open for GOD, watch for his works; / be alert for signs of his presence. / Remember the world of wonders he has made, / his miracles and the verdicts he's rendered— / O seed of Abraham, his servant . . . . / . . . [H]e remembers, remembers his Covenant— / for a thousand generations he's been as good as his word. / It's the Covenant he made with Abraham . . . ." (Ps 105:1–6a, 8–9a, TM)

RESULTS

Scripture: ". . . [S]ince we are justified by faith, we have peace with God through our Lord Jesus Christ, through whom we have obtained access to this grace in which we stand, and we boast in our hope of sharing the glory of God. For while we were still weak, at the right time Christ died for the ungodly. . . . God proves his love for us in that while we still were sinners Christ died for us. Much more surely, therefore, since we have now been justified by his blood, will we be saved through him . . . . For if while we were enemies we were reconciled to God through the death of his Son, much more surely, having been reconciled, will we be saved by his life." (Rom 5:1–2, 6, 8–10, NRSVue)

Reflection: Because people have been made righteous by a divine gift, Paul urges that they make the necessary response and take advantage of his offer. The result will be peace, achieved by Jesus Anointed. People are no longer separated from God; they have been reconciled through grace in which they now stand. They have access to God's love in an impartial form. This leads them to boast in their hope of sharing the glory of God—the awe that was manifest in holiness and power to create and redeem. While trapped in Adam's sin, the Anointed One died for all undeserving sinners. Then, according to Paul, such justification achieved by Jesus' blood on the cross, demonstrates not only God's love, but his desire that all be saved through him. If reconciliation with God was achieved while people were sinner-enemies, how much more does future salvation await those who accept the divine gift.

Meditation/Journal: What has the access to grace through Jesus Anointed accomplished in you? In what specific ways has God showed his love to you?

Psalm Response: "Sing GOD a brand-new song! / Earth and everyone in it, sing! / Sing to GOD—worship GOD! / Take the news of his glory to the lost, / News of his wonders to one and all! / For GOD is great, and worth a thousand Hallelujahs. / Bravo, GOD, Bravo! / Everyone join in the great shout: Encore! / In awe before the beauty, in awe before the might." (Ps 96:1–4, 7, TM)

ADAM AND ANOINTED ONE

Scripture: ". . . [J]ust as sin came into the world through one man, and death came through sin, and so death spread to all because all have sinned . . . . Yet death reigned from Adam to Moses, even over those who did not sin in the likeness of Adam, who is a pattern of the one who was to come. . . . If the many died through the one man's trespass, much more surely have the grace of God and the gift in the grace of the one man, Jesus Christ, abounded for the many. If because of the one man's trespass, death reigned through that one, much more surely will those who receive the abundance of grace and the gift of righteousness reign in life through the one man, Jesus Christ. Therefore just as one man's trespass led to condemnation for all, so one's man's act of righteousness leads to justification and life for all." (Rom 5:12, 14, 15b, 17–18, NRSVue)

Reflection: In his First Letter to the Corinthians, Paul wrote, ". . . [S]ince death came through a human, the resurrection of the dead has also come through a human, for as all die in Adam, so all will be made alive in Christ" (1 Cor 15:21–22, NRSVue). Just as Adam's life defined the future of his descendants, now Christ's life defines the future destiny of believers. Using the story in the HB (OT) book of Genesis (3:1–24), which explains the origin of sin, Paul states that death came as a result of Adam's fall. Adam's transgression-act determined the fate of his descendants; the Anointed's grace-gift-act redetermined the fate of all believers. The Anointed's redemptive work had the power to overcome Adam's legacy. In other words, the reign of death initiated by Adam is surpassed and overturned by the new reign of those accepting grace and righteousness in the Anointed. It is the abundant life in the Anointed that overturns the legacy of sin and death. God makes believers right with himself through their acceptance of the gospel of the Anointed crucified and raised. Therefore, a new realm of abundant life has been brought into being now and into the future. In his First Letter to the Corinthians, Paul states it this way: "The first man, Adam, became a living being; the last Adam became a life-giving spirit" (12 Cor 15:45, NRSVue). Looking toward the future, Paul writes, "Just as we have borne the image of the one of dust [Adam], we will also bear the image of the one of heaven [Christ]" (1 Cor 15:49, NRSVue). With Paul we can say, "Thanks be to God, who gives us the victory through our Lord Jesus Christ." (1 Cor 15:57, NRSVue). It is important to note that in Paul's thought the future is not based on human qualifications or performance; it depends totally on God.

Meditation/Journal: According to Paul, who is the originator of death? According to Paul, who is the originator of life? Do you agree or disagree? Why? Now, how do you experience the life-giving spirit?

Psalm Response: "Sing to GOD a brand-new song. / He's made a world of wonders! / He rolled up his sleeves, / He set things right. / GOD made history with salvation, / He showed the world what he could do. / He remembered to love us, a bonus / To his dear family, . . . indefatigable love. / Shout your praises to GOD, everybody! / Let loose and sing! Strike up the band!" (Ps 98:1–4, TM)

BAPTISM

Scripture: ". . . [W]here sin increased, grace abounded all the more, so that, just as sin reigned in death, so grace might also reign through justification leading to eternal life through Jesus Christ our Lord. Should we continue in sin in order that grace may increase? By no means! Do you not know that all of us who were baptized into Christ Jesus were baptized into his death? Therefore we were buried with him by baptism into death, so that, just as Christ was raised from the dead by the glory of the Father, so we also might walk in newness of life. For if we have been united with him in a death like his, we will certainly be united with him in a resurrection like his." (Rom 5:20–21; 6:1–2a, 3–5, NRSVue)

Reflection: Paul's effort to demote the role of Torah as being out of control is best emphasized in his Letter to the Galatians. He writes, ". . . [I]f a law had been given that could make alive, then righteousness would indeed come through the law" (Gal 3:21c, NRSVue). In Paul's view, the time for Torah has passed; it has been surpassed by Jesus Anointed, who has set free believers. If, as Paul states, that grace has abounded, overwhelming sin, the logical conclusion is that people should sin more in order to activate more grace! Paul dismisses that illogical conclusion. He understands the event of Jesus' crucifixion as revealing the superabundance of grace. Grace conquered death; God raised Jesus from the dead. Those who have been baptized into the Anointed Jesus are immersed into his death, and like him, they have been made righteous, appropriating the death of the Anointed for themselves. In his Second Letter to the Corinthians, Paul explains this: ". . . [W]e are convinced that one has died for all; therefore all have died" (2 Cor 5:14, NRSVue).

Baptism is participation in the death of the Anointed. Thus, it is no longer the baptized person who lives, but it is the Anointed who lives in him or her (Gal 2:19–20). Paul claims that believers were co-buried with Jesus Anointed in a baptismal shared grave. And like God raised his Anointed from the dead to new life, believers in the Anointed constitute a new creation (2 Cor 5:17; Gal 6:15). All believers form a unity with the Anointed, already sharing in the new life of grace. Paul's statement about hope in the future is that what God did for the Anointed he will do for all believers; it is God's gift for the future.

Meditation/Journal: In what specific ways have you experienced being crucified with Jesus Anointed? In what specific ways have you experienced being a new creation?

Psalm Response: "I'm proud to praise God, / proud to praise GOD. / Fearless now, I trust in God; / what can mere mortals do to me? / God, you did everything you promised, / and I'm thanking you with all my heart. / You pulled me from the brink of death, / my feet from the cliff-edge of doom. / Now I stroll at leisure with God / in the sunlit fields of life." (Ps 57:10–13, TM)

LAW

Scripture: ". . . [Y]ou have died to the law through the body of Christ, so that you may belong to another, to him who was raised from the dead in order that we may bear fruit for God. For while we were living in the flesh, our sinful passions, aroused by the law, were at work in our members to bear fruit for death. But now we are discharged from the law, dead to that which held us captive, so that we are enslaved in the newness of the Spirit and not in the oldness of the written code." (Rom 7:4–6, NRSVue)

Reflection: The above passage explains Paul's perspective concerning Torah, the 613 precepts of the law. The purpose of the law was to identify sin (Rom 3:20). However, through baptism (Rom 6:4), believers died with the crucified Anointed (Rom 6:2–6). They were incorporated into the event of the Anointed's death and released from the bondage of Torah. God has acted through the death and resurrection of the incorporated Anointed that brings the era of Torah to an end, and, through baptism, ushers believers into a new era of grace. "[A]nyone united to the Lord becomes one spirit with him" (1 Cor 6:17, NRSVue). For Paul there is an antithesis between flesh and spirit. While living in the flesh, the sinful passions were aroused by Torah, bearing fruit for death. Now, believers have been set free from Torah, but they are enslaved by the newness of the Spirit. Paul's words about being set free from Torah represent a radical break from Paul's traditional Judaism. Believers serve the Anointed not by keeping Torah, but by following the Spirit; "the fruit of the Spirit is love, joy, peace, patience, kindness, generosity, faithfulness, gentleness, and self-control" (Gal 5:22–23, NRSVue). In his Second Letter to the Corinthians, Paul refers to this way of life as "a new covenant, not of letter but of spirit, for the letter kills, but the Spirit gives life." (2 Cor 3:6, NRSVue).

Meditation/Journal: To whom do you belong? What process did you go through to belong to him or her? What fruit has your relationship borne?

Psalm Response: "How well God must like you— / . . . you thrill to GOD's Word, / you chew on Scripture day and night. / You're a tree replanted in Eden, / bearing fresh fruit every month, / Never dropping a leaf, / always in blossom. / GOD charts the road you take. (Ps 1:1–3, 6a, TM)

SPIRIT-WALKING

Scripture: ". . . God has done what the law, weakened by the flesh, could not do by sending his own Son in the likeness of sinful flesh and to deal with sin, he condemned sin in the flesh, so that the just requirement of the law might be fulfilled in us, who walk not according to the flesh but according to the Spirit. . . . [W]e are obligated, not to the flesh, to live according to the flesh—for if you live according to the flesh, you will die, but if by the Spirit you put to death the deeds of the body, you will live." (Rom 8:3–4, 12–13, NRSVue)

Reflection: In Pauline thought, flesh refers to the sinful corporality of the body. What Torah could not do for the flesh, God did by sending his Son as a human being. Through Jesus' death, God condemned sin by destroying his body, and, thus cancelling sin— what the law could not do. Jesus Anointed took the likeness of sinful flesh to free people from sin and to open the possibility of new life in the Spirit. In his Second Letter to the Corinthians, Paul states it this way: "For our sake God made the one who knew no sin to be sin, so that in him we might become the righteousness of God" (2 Cor 5:21). Now, we walk according to the Spirit; lifestyle is now dictated by the Spirit, not by Torah. The Pauline antithesis between flesh and Spirit is expressed in the Letter to the Galatians: "Live by the Spirit, I say, and do not gratify the desires of the flesh. For what the flesh desires is opposed to the Spirit, and what the Spirit desires is opposed to the flesh, for these are opposed to each other . . . . [I]f you are led by the Spirit, you are not subject to the law" (Gal 5:16–18, NRSVue). Living according to the lifestyle of the flesh results in death; but living according to the lifestyle of the Spirit, putting to death the deeds of the body (flesh), results in life. The Spirit of God, who raised Jesus from the dead, leads those who have been baptized into his death and resurrection. Being led by that same Spirit is to be constrained by divine intervention, a compelling spiritual force guiding the steps of all walkers.

Meditation/Journal: In what specific ways do you walk according to the Spirit? What specific elements of your lifestyle are prompted by the Spirit? by the flesh?

Psalm Response: "I've thrown in my lot with you, GOD, and / I'm not budging. / Examine me, GOD, from head to foot, / order your battery of tests. / Make sure I'm fit / inside and out / So I never lose / sight of your love, / But keep in step with you, / never missing a beat. / (Ps 26:1b–3, TM)

GLORIFIED

Scripture: "We know that all things work together for good for those who love God, who are called according to his purpose. For those whom he foreknew he also predestined to be conformed to the image of his Son, in order that he might be the firstborn within a large family. And those whom he predestined he also called, and those whom he called he also justified, and those whom he justified he also glorified." (Rom 8:28–30, NRSVue)

Reflection: Divine activity leads to good results for those who love God in response to the event—death and resurrection—of Jesus Anointed. The Spirit works with those who love God to achieve the divine purpose. God calls believers; the response of believers is demonstratable in their actions. Their lifestyle has been transformed in baptism in which an old self was buried and a new self raised. The process of transformation continues as believers cooperate with the Spirit to achieve God's purpose. Jesus Anointed recovered the divine image that had been lost to sin and became the firstborn among many siblings who do likewise. The Anointed's mission was to restore the image of God, who predestined people to respond to the gospel and share in the righteousness of God. Believers are in the process of being glorified according to the image of the Anointed. "[The Lord Jesus Christ] will transform the body of our humiliation, that it may be conformed to the body of his glory . . . ," writes Paul to the Philippians (3:21). In his Second Letter to the Corinthians, Paul writes: ". . . [A]ll of us . . . seeing the glory of the Lord as though reflected in a mirror, are being transformed into the same image from one degree of glory to another, for this comes from the Lord, the Spirit" (2 Cor 3:18).

Meditation/Journal: What is God's purpose for you? What recent transformation has occurred in your life? What degree of glory do you recognize in your life?

Psalm Response: "O LORD, our Sovereign, / how majestic is your name in all the earth! / You have set your glory above the heavens. / [W]hat are human beings that you are mindful of them, / mortals that you care for them? / Yet you have made them a little lower than God, / and crowned them with glory and honor." (Ps 8:1, 4–5, NRSV)

NO SEPARATION

Scripture: "If God is for us, who is against us? He who did not withhold his own Son but gave him up for all of us how will he not with him also give us everything else? Who will bring any charge against God's elect? It is God who justifies. Who is to condemn? It is Christ who died, or rather, who was raised, who is also at the right hand of God, who also intercedes for us. Who will separate us from the love of Christ? Will affliction or distress or persecution or famine or nakedness or peril or sword? . . . [I]n all these things we are more than victorious through him who loved us. For I am convinced that neither death, nor life, nor angels, nor rulers, nor things present, nor things to come, nor powers, nor height, nor depth, nor anything else in all creation will be able to separate us from the love of God in Christ Jesus our Lord." (Rom 8:31b–35, 37–39, NRSVue)

Reflection: For Paul, God's saving act in Jesus Anointed characterizes God, who is for people. Because God demonstrated that he is for people through the death and resurrection of his Son, no one can change that favor. In other words, no one can prevail against God. If God willed to give his own Son—his greatest gift—he will also give people everything else. In other words, God's reluctance to spare his own Son is the ultimate act a Father could perform on behalf of others; clearly, nothing more demonstrates that God is for people. While people do not deserve (nor can they earn) so great a gift, God chooses people, like he chose Jesus Anointed, and makes them righteous. Thus, people can be assured, according to Paul, that nothing can separate them from the Anointed's love, which gives them a glimpse of God's love. Just like God seated his Son at his right hand of power, he promises to do the same for people. No adversity—affliction, distress, persecution, famine, nakedness (destitution), peril, or sword (death, capital punishment)—can separate people from the love of the Anointed. Walking through such adversity is a sign of discipleship. According to Paul, those who are true disciples of the Anointed are super-victors through love, derived from the power of the gospel, which declares that

God is revealed in the Anointed's death and resurrection. Therefore, nothing—death, life, angels (spiritual forces), rulers, things
present, things to come, power (fate), height, or depth—can separate people from the love of God in Anointed Jesus. In other words,
nothing can succeed in severing the relationship between people
and God. The Anointed, who reveals divine love, is Lord over all
powers in heaven and on earth; the motivating center is love.

Meditation/Journal: What do you think (believe) separates you
from the love of God in Christ? How is that possible?

Psalm Response: "I've thrown in my lot with you, GOD, and /
I'm not budging. / Make sure I'm fit / inside and out / So I never
lose / sight of your love, / But keep in step with you, / never missing a beat. / GOD, I love living with you; / your house glows with
your glory. / You know I've been aboveboard with you; / now be
aboveboard with me. / I'm on the level with you, GOD; / I bless
you every chance I get." (Ps 26:1b, 2b–3, 8, 11–12, TM)

MERCY

Scripture: "Is there injustice on God's part? By no means! For he
says to Moses, 'I will have mercy on whom I have mercy, / and I
will have compassion on whom I have compassion.' So it depends
not on human will or exertion but on God who shows mercy. So
then he has mercy on whomever he chooses, and he hardens the
heart of whomever he chooses." (Rom 9:14b–16, 18, NRSVue)

Reflection: Paul illustrates a presupposition of biblical understanding that is nearly lost on most Bible readers. That presupposition
is God is in charge of the world he created. After discussing biblical issues that illustrate that God chooses some people over others
(even hardening their hearts), Paul asks his readers if that implies
that God is unjust. The question is about God's basic fairness in
dealing with people. As he usually does, the apostle declares that it
does not imply that God is unjust. According to Paul, it is primarily a matter of mercy. To make his point he quotes the Hebrew
Bible (Old Testament) book of Exodus (33:19), where God makes
clear that he bestows divine benefits on whomever he calls; one

cannot earn or be privileged to divine benefits. They are a divine decision. In other words, God is free to show mercy. According to Paul, it is because God is merciful that he has made justification by faith possible. Divine mercy is sovereign. Thus, for Paul, the truly scandalous form of selectivity is that God has mercy on whomever he wills—those who do not deserve it.

Meditation/Journal: What mercy has God showed you? In a culture based on fairness (justice), what are the consequences of Paul's words about God showing mercy on whomever he chooses?

Psalm Response: "I look to you, heaven-dwelling God, / I look up to you for help. / Like servants, alert to their master's commands, / like a maiden attending her lady, / We're watching and waiting, holding our breath, / awaiting your word of mercy. / Mercy, GOD, mercy! (Ps 123:1–3, TM)

FAITH VS. WORKS

Scripture: "Gentiles, who did not strive for righteousness, have attained it, that is, righteousness through faith, but Israel, who did strive for the law of righteousness, did not attain that law. Why not? Because they did not strive for it on the basis of faith but as if it were based on works. (Rom 9:30–32b, NRSVue)

Reflection: In the above passage from Paul's Letter to the Romans, he deals with the present situation of the Jews; they fail to recognize the Anointed as the goal of Torah; in Christ there is righteousness for everyone who has faith. Paul presents an ironic antithesis between Gentiles, who received righteousness through faith without working for it, while Jews strove for it, but did not achieve it. Gentiles were responding positively to the gospel of grace: a free gift (Rom 1:16–17; 3:21–31; 4:1–25). However, in Paul's view, Jews thought that it was through human achievement (works) that righteousness was achieved. In his Letter to the Galatians, he puts it this way: ". . . [W]e know that a person is justified not by the works of the law but through the faith of Jesus Christ. And we have come to believe in Christ Jesus, so that we might be justified by the faith of Christ and not by doing the works of the law, because no one will be justified by the works of the law" (Gal 2:16, NRSVue). In other words, the Jews (Israelites) failed to achieve righteousness through obedience to Torah; in that statement there is an echo of Paul describing his life before his conversion (Phil 3:5–6). For Paul, a person cannot accomplish his or her own righteousness, even as it is embedded in Torah, because it becomes opposition to the Anointed. The Jews' error, in Pauline thought, is the refusal to accept faith in the Anointed. Torah and works, which refer to the Jewish way of life, cannot be accepted by Gentiles (especially the work of circumcision). Through the Anointed, God, who had given Torah to the Jews (Hebrews, Israelites), decided to offer righteousness to all people: Gentiles and Jews. According to Paul, God was offering his mercy and salvation to both Gentiles and Jews.

Meditation/Journal: What specific roles do faith and works play in your lifestyle? Are you more like the Jews, attempting to earn righteousness through Torah works, or are you more like the Gentiles, accepting God's offer of righteousness through faith? Explain.

Psalm Response: "I waited and waited and waited for GOD. / At last he looked; finally he listened. / Blessed are you who give yourselves over to GOD, / turn your backs on the world's 'sure thing,' / ignore what the world worships . . . . / . . . God's Word entered my life, / became part of my very being. / I've preached you [, God,] to the whole congregation, / I've kept back nothing, GOD—you know that. / I didn't keep the news of your ways / a secret, didn't keep it to myself. / I told it all, how dependable you are, how thorough, / I didn't hold back pieces of love and truth / For myself alone. I told it all, / let the congregation know the whole story." (Ps 40:1, 4, 8–10, TM)

PRAYING FOR SALVATION

Scripture: "Brothers and sisters, my heart's desire and prayer to God for [the Jews] is that they may be saved. For I can testify that they have a zeal for God, but it is not based on knowledge. Not knowing the righteousness of God and seeking to establish their own, they have not submitted to God's righteousness. For Christ is the culmination of the law so that there may be righteousness for everyone who believes." (Rom 10:1–4, NRSVue)

Reflection: The above passage begins with a personal tone; Paul has a personal relationship with the Jews (Israel). He is one of them, and he possesses a deep concern for the salvation of his kinsfolk. Out of his heart's good pleasure, he prays for them. Because he is Jewish (Gal 1:14; Phil 3:6), he has experienced their passionate, consuming desire to do God's will (Torah), but even with such fervent commitment—such inward state of being—they do not know God; they are ignorant of his righteousness and seek to establish their own righteousness. In Paul's understanding, they need to submit to God's righteousness as revealed in the gospel; God's righteousness is granted by grace alone and not by Torah. God's Anointed reveals and fulfills the goal of Torah, which, over time, had been subverted. In the Anointed, God's righteousness was offered to all who believe in the gospel, both Jews and Greeks. Thus, Paul's broken heart and his prayer is that his fellow Jews will see the bigger picture and accept the gift God was offering to them and to the Gentiles.

Meditation/Journal: In what recent experience of your life have you seen the bigger picture, when the members of your family or group were stuck in the smaller picture? What knowledge was missing? Did others submit? Why? Why not?

Psalm Response: "I'm determined to watch steps and tongue / so they won't land me in trouble. / I decided to hold my tongue . . . . / 'Mum's the word,' I said, and kept quiet. / But the longer I kept silence / The worse it got— / my insides got hotter and hotter. / My thoughts boiled over; / I spilled my guts. / 'Ah, GOD, listen to my prayer, my / cry—open your ears. / Don't be callous; / just look at these tears of mine. / I'm a stranger here. I don't know my way— / a migrant like my whole family. / Give me a break, cut me some slack / before it's too late and I'm out of here.'" (Ps 39:1–3, 12–13, TM)

SALVATION FOR ALL

Scripture: "... [I]f you confess with your mouth that Jesus is Lord and believe in your heart that God raised him from the dead, you will be saved. For one believes with the heart, leading to righteousness, and one confesses with the mouth, leading to salvation. For there is no distinction between Jew and Greek; the same Lord is Lord of all and is generous to all who call on him." (Rom 10:9–10, 12, NRSVue)

Reflection: "Jesus is Lord" or "Lord Jesus" is an early expression of allegiance to the Anointed. Parallels can be found in Paul's First Letter to the Corinthians (1:2; 12:3) and in his Letter to the Philippians (2:11). The phrase does not indicate the Anointed's divine status; it is focused on the believer's identity and commitment. In other words, it binds the believer in loyalty to the Anointed, and denotes an attitude of subserviency to him. A believer believes in the heart, the center of humans where the deepest of convictions are held, that God raised Jesus from the dead. Preaching as done by Paul leads to the acceptance of God's offer of righteousness, and that evokes the oral confession that "Jesus is Lord." Salvation is deliverance from sin. All who participate in the process—preaching, believe, confession—no matter be they Jews or Gentiles are saved. Furthermore, the boundaries between Jews and Gentiles have been erased; there are no longer distinctions; in other words, the gospel removes prejudicial boundaries; the Anointed is sovereign universally; through him God has established a new realm of plenitude (generosity) in which all are treated equally. The riches of the divine favor have been bestowed impartially upon all who call on him.

Meditation/Journal: What is your response to Paul's statement that through Jesus Christ, God has offered salvation to all?

Psalm Response: "Light, space, zest— / that's GOD! / So, with him on my side I'm fearless, / afraid of no one and nothing. / Listen, GOD, I'm calling at the top of my lungs: 'Be good to me! Answer me!' / When my heart whispered, 'Seek God,' / my whole being replied, 'I'm seeking him!' / Don't hide from me now. / You've always been right there for me; / don't turn your back on me now. / Don't throw me out, don't abandon me; / you've always kept the door open." (Ps 27:1, 7–9, TM)

REJECTION?

Scripture: ". . . [H]as God rejected his people? By no means! I myself am an Israelite, a descendant of Abraham, a member of the tribe of Benjamin. God has not rejected his people whom he foreknew. . . . [A]t the present time there is a remnant chosen by grace. But if it is by grace, it is no longer on the basis of works, otherwise grace would no longer be grace." (Rom 11:1–2a, 5–6, NRSVue)

Reflection: This section of Paul's Letter to the Romans clearly indicates that the letter was meant as oral communication; someone who was literate read the letter, pausing after the questions, so the listeners could respond, hopefully, in the way Paul wanted! Paul presents himself as an example that his people have not been abandoned by God. He identifies himself as thoroughly Jewish: an Israelite, a descendant of Abraham, a member of the tribe of Benjamin, from which came Israel's first king, Saul, after whom Paul was named. It is inconceivable that God would change his mind about the people he had chosen; if such were the case, God would be presented as whimsical, not true to the covenant he initiated with Abraham. In his Letter to the Galatians, Paul reminds his readers: "You have heard, no doubt, of my earlier life in Judaism. I was violently persecuting the church of God and was trying to destroy it" (Gal 1:13, NRSVue). However, now the one "who formerly was persecuting [the church]" was "proclaiming the faith he once tried to destroy" (Gal 1:23, NRSVue), and nothing could hinder him "from speaking to the gentiles so that they may be saved" (1 Thess 2:16, NRSVue). Because God, in Pauline thought, knows his people even before they are born, he has not reneged on his people. In fact, he has seen to it that a remnant, some people, have survived, while many were killed in battle or exiled. Those believers were chosen by God according to the principle of grace;

such divine benefaction or unconditional access to God comes with benefits to the underserving through the Anointed.

Meditation/Journal: What is grace? In what specific ways have you experienced it?

Psalm Response: "Hallelujah! / You who serve GOD, praise GOD! / Just to speak his name is praise! / Just to remember GOD is a blessing— / now and tomorrow and always. / From east to west, from dawn to dusk, / keep lifting all your praises to GOD! / God is higher than anything and anyone, / outshining everything you can see in the skies. / Who can compare with GOD, our God, / so majestically enthroned, / Surveying his magnificent / heavens and earth?" (Ps 113:1–6, TM)

STUMBLING

Scripture: "So I ask, have [the Jews] stumbled so as to fall? By no means! But through their stumbling salvation has come to the gentiles, so as to make Israel jealous. Now if their stumbling means riches for the world and if their loss means riches for gentiles, how much more will their full inclusion mean! I celebrate my ministry in order to make my own people jealous and thus save some of them. For it their rejection is the reconciliation of the world, what will their acceptance be but life from the dead?" (Rom 11:11–12, 13b–15, NRSVue)

Reflection: In the above passage, Paul continues to reflect upon his own people, Israel (Jews). He asks his readers if they think that the Jews have stumbled to fall. He answers no. Instead of understanding stumbling as a negative event, Paul sees it in a positive light. The Jewish rejection of the gospel is clear, but God did not intend the destruction of his people. As far as Paul is concerned, God's intent was the salvation of the Gentiles in order to provoke the Jews to zeal. The benefits given to the Gentiles come through the resistance of the Jews, and the conversion of the Gentiles will provoke the Jews to a reaction that will result in their conversion. Whereas a stumbling was presumed to lead to failure, in Pauline thought it, paradoxically, brings reconciliation and life. All human expectations are overturned. The ultimate conversion of the Jews, according to Paul, belongs to his office as apostle to the Gentiles.

Meditation/Journal: From your life experiences choose one where you stumbled in some way. Did you see your stumbling negatively or positively? Explain. What purpose did your stumbling have?

Psalm Response: "Open up before GOD, keep nothing back; / he'll do whatever needs to be done: / He'll validate your life in the clear light of day / and stamp you with approval at high noon. / Quiet down before GOD, / be prayerful before him. / Stalwart walks in step with GOD; / his path blazed by GOD, he's happy. / If he stumbles, he's not down for long; / GOD has a grip on his hand." (Ps 37:5–7a, 23–24, TM)

OLIVE TREE

Scripture: ". . . [I]f some of the [Jewish] branches [of the olive tree] were broken off, and you [, Gentiles,] a wild olive shoot, were grafted among the others to share the rich root of the olive tree, do not boast over the branches. If you do boast, remember you do not support the root, but the root supports you. You will say, 'Branches were broken off so that I might be grafted in.' That is true. They were broken off on account of unbelief, but you stand on account of belief. So do not become arrogant, but be afraid. For if God did not spare the natural branches, neither will he spare you. (Rom 11:17–21, NRSVue)

Reflection: Paul employs the image of an olive tree in chapter 12 of his Letter to the Romans. The reader knew that wild olive trees were better described as small, scraggly bushes that produced nothing useful! Branches from tame (cultivated) olive trees could be grafted onto wild ones to produce abundant fruit. In Paul's analogy, the wild olive branches are the Gentiles, who have been grafted into the cultivated Jewish tree with solid roots. This implies that the grafted branches are equal sharers in holy life. In fact, some of the cultivated branches have been broken off by God for this to take place. As Paul makes clear, it is the Jewish root that supports the Gentile branches. The Jews cannot boast, because the grafting of the Gentiles branches is one of God's deeds. And the Gentiles cannot boast, because that is another one of God's gracious deeds. Salvation exists because of Israel. According to Paul, the reason some Jewish branches were removed from the olive tree was because of their unbelief and to make room for the Gentile branches to be grafted on and flourish. There is no room for boasting. If God didn't spare some of the natural branches on the olive tree (the Jews), God will not spare the Gentile branches he has grafted in their place, if they begin to boast. God has the final authority, the final word, as to which branches are growing on his olive tree.

Journal/Meditation: Are you a natural branch or a grafted-on branch on the olive tree? Explain. Specifically, what gets in your way of seeing all the branches on the olive tree as equal sharers of the life that comes from the root?

Psalm Response: "Why do you brag of evil, 'Big Man'? / God's mercy carries the day. / God will tear you limb from limb, / sweep you up and throw you out, / Pull you up by the roots / from the land of life. / And I'm an olive tree, / growing green in God's house. / I trusted in the generous mercy / of God then and now. / I thank you always / that you went into action. / And I'll stay right here, / your good name my hope, / in company with your faithful friends." (Ps 52:1, 5, 8–9, TM)

GRAFT

Scripture: ". . . [E]ven those of Israel, if they do not continue in unbelief, will be grafted in, for God has the power to graft them in again. For if you have been cut from what is by nature a wild olive tee and grafted, contrary to nature, into a cultivated olive tree, how much more will these natural branches be grafted into their own olive tree." (Rom 11:23–24, NRSVue)

Reflection: According to Paul in his Letter to the Romans, Israel's fall (disbelief) will be overcome by divine power. Continuing to use the image of the olive tree, he reflects on the process of grafting wild olive tree branches onto cultivated olive trees. The groups of Jews (branches cut off by God) resisting the gospel Paul preaches

44

will end up grafted alongside the Gentiles on the one olive tree, if they cease their unbelief. God is able to graft them back onto the cultivated olive tree. As he writes in his Second Letter to the Corinthians, ". . . God is able to provide you with every blessing in abundance, so that by always having enough of everything, you may share abundantly in every good work" (2 Cor 9:8, NRSVue). Grace transforms and breaks through resistance (as it did for the Gentiles). If wild olive branches (Gentiles) can be grafted divinely onto the cultivated olive tree, how much more will divine grace regraft natural branches onto the cultivated olive tree! Then, all equal branches will share in the benefits of the one tree. According to Paul, God intends to have only one, holy, sacred tree.

Meditation/Journal: When have you, like a wild or cultivated olive branch, experienced being grafted onto a cultivated olive tree (group, committee, etc.)? Explain.

Psalm Response: "GOD, my God, how great you are! / beautifully, gloriously robed, / Dressed up in sunshine, / and all heaven stretched out for your tent. / GOD's trees are well-watered— / Birds build their nests in those trees . . . . / What a wildly wonderful world, GOD! / You made it all, with Wisdom at your side, / made earth overflow with your wonderful creations." (Ps 104:1b–2, 16a, 17a, 24, TM)

HARDENING

Scripture: ". . . [A] hardening has come upon part of Israel until the full number of the gentiles has come in. And in this way all Israel will be saved . . . . As regards the gospel [Gentiles] are enemies for your sake, but as regards election they are beloved for the sake of their ancestors, for the gifts and the calling of God are irrevocable. Just as you were once disobedient to God but have now received mercy because of their disobedience, so also they have now been disobedient in order that, by the mercy shown to you, they also may now receive mercy. For God has imprisoned all in disobedience so that he may be merciful to all. O the depth of the riches and wisdom and knowledge of God! How unsearchable are his judgments and how inscrutable his ways!" (Rom 11:25–26, 28–33, NRSVue)

Reflection: Because God is in charge of everything in Pauline thought, Paul can write that his own people's disbelief (hardening) is God's work. Paul has in mind God's hardening of Pharaoh's heart in the Hebrew Bible (Old Testament) book of Exodus (4:21; 7:3, 13–14, 22; 8:15, 19, 32; 9:7, 12, 34–35; 10:1, 20, 27; 11:10; 14:4, 8, 17). The author reduces both Gentiles and Jews to the level of disobedience in order to illustrate that both groups have received divine mercy, which triumphs over all. Some Jewish hearts have been hardened by God for the sake of the conversion of the Gentiles. However, in time that malady will be overcome when all the Gentiles predestined to believe do believe. God's act of hardening Jewish hearts does not, according to Paul, imply that God has rejected some of his people. God's gifts and calling are irrevocable; if they are revocable, then God is wishy-washy, and there is nothing to prevent him from changing his mind again! On the contrary, God is rich in mercy; thus, according to Paul, he has made some Jews and Gentiles disobedient (hardened) so that he can lavish his mercy upon all of them. In other words, there is only one, cultivated olive tree (Israel) with both Jews and Gentiles grafted onto it. The obtuseness of some Jews is, according to Paul, to provide time for the Gentiles. Whereas in the past, God chose the Jews, now he has chosen both Gentiles and Jews (all). God's faithfulness remains firm. God's mercy is sovereign; salvation is a matter of grace and not any form of human achievement. The Jews will be saved in the same way as the Gentiles: as a result of God's mercy. After explaining that Pauline insight, Paul breaks into an exclamation of praise, a hymn, which explores the inexhaustible and unsearchable fullness of God.

Meditation/Journal: What is your response to Paul's understanding that God has everything under control? to Paul's words about God hardening some Jewish hearts? to Paul's words about the reason God hardened some Jewish hearts? to Paul's words about God's mercy.

Canticle Response: "Is there anyone around who can explain God? / Anyone smart enough to tell him what to do? / Anyone who has done him such a huge favor that God has to ask his advice? / Everything comes from him; / Everything happens through him; / Everything ends up in him. / Always glory! Always praise! / Yes, Yes. Yes." (Rom 11:34–36, TM)

ONE BODY

Scripture: ". . . [A]s in one body we have many members and not all the members have the same function, so we, who are many, are one body in Christ, and individually we are members one of another. We have gifts that differ according to the grace given to us . . . ." (Rom 12:4–6, NRSVue)

Reflection: Paul's metaphor of the body is one known by many people because it also appears in his First Letter to the Corinthians, and in second generation Pauline letters features Christ as its head (Eph 4:12; Col 1:18). Paul has in mind the human body with its many members: eyes, ears, nose, mouth, fingers, legs, feet, toes, etc. Just as the many members of a human body do not have the same function, so are many people in the one body of the Anointed. Paul's focus is on unity; he understands that each individual believer is a member of all other believers. In other words, all members are interdependent. ". . . [J]ust as the body is one and has many members, and all the members of the body, though many, are one body, so it is with Christ," he writes in his First Letter to the Corinthians (12:12, NRSVue). Each believer possesses some gift, some grace, from God; the gift is a manifestation of God and belongs to the whole body. Paul lists seven of those gifts. In his First Letter to the Corinthians, he explains more of what he means and gives examples. "Indeed, the body does not consist of one member but of many" (1 Cor 12:14, NRSVue). According to Paul, "God has so arranged the body . . . that there may be no dissension within the body, but the members may have the same care for one another" (1 Cor 12:24–25, NRSVue). Recognizing that unity results of diversity, Paul tells the Corinthians, as he does the

Romans, "you are the body of Christ and individually members of it" (1 Cor 12:27, NRSVue).

Meditation/Journal: Characterize yourself as a member of the body of Christ. What gift (grace) has God given to you for the good of the other members? Explain.

Psalm Response: "God, mark us with grace / and blessing! Smile! / The whole country will see how your work . . . . / God! Let people thank and enjoy you. / Let all people thank and enjoy you. / Earth, display your exuberance! / You mark us with blessing, O God, our God. / You mark us with blessing, O God. / Earth's four corners— honor him!" (Ps 67:1, 3, 6–7, TM)

OWE

Scripture: "Owe no one anything, except to love one another, for the one who loves another has fulfilled the law. Love does no wrong to a neighbor; therefore, love is the fulfilling of the law." (Rom 13:8, 10, NRSVue)

Reflection: In Pauline understanding, there is value in being free from debts, either monetary or social. Paul wants believers to be free so they can devote themselves to their new obligation: to be indebted only to mutual agape (love that puts the other ahead of oneself). In his Letter to the Galatians, he tells his readers: ". . . [Y]ou were called to freedom . . . only do not use your freedom as an opportunity for self-indulgence, but through love become en- slaved to one another. For the whole law is summed up in a single commandment, 'You shall love your neighbor as yourself'" (Gal 5:13–14, NRSVue). Love between fellow believers accomplishes the original intent of Torah and beyond in the everyday experi- ence of living in small groups of believers. The love that should exist within the community (neighbor) stops those who love from wronging their neighbors in any way. To do evil to the neighbor is, in fact, to do evil to oneself. The purpose of Torah is fulfilled when people are willing to sacrifice themselves for each other.

Meditation/Journal: In your experience, how do debts get in the way of love? In your experience how does paying off debts free you to love others sacrificially?

Psalm Response: "GOD, who gets invited / to dinner at your place? / How do we get on your guest list? / 'Walk straight, / act right, tell the truth. / Don't hurt your friend, / don't blame your neighbor; / despise the despicable. / Keep your word even when it costs you, / make an honest living, / never take a bribe. / You'll never get / blacklisted / if you live like this'" (Ps 15:1–5, TM)

AWAKEN

Scripture: ". . . [Y]ou know what time it is, how it is already the moment for you to wake from sleep. For salvation is nearer to us now than when we became believers; the night is far gone; the day is near. Let us then throw off the works of darkness and put on the armor of light . . . ." (Rom 13:11–12, NRSVue)

Reflection: According to Paul, the final age had come for those who believed that God raised from the dead Jesus Anointed. The moment had arrived for them to live in the new reality of the Anointed's realm; the new age of salvation was present. Thus, it was high time for believers to become aware that they were living in the divine plan begun with the death and resurrection of the Anointed, while they awaited the time of his return (Parousia). In Pauline thought, that event was coming soon; it is like the time between the end of night and the beginning of dawn; the light is near; the Parousia is near! In his First Letter to the Thessalonians, he writes: ". . . [Y]ou . . . are not in darkness, for that day to surprise you like a thief, for you are all children of light and children of the day; we are not of the night or of darkness. So, then let us not fall asleep as other do, but let us keep awake . . . ." (1 Thess 5:4–6, NRSVue). Believers are exhorted to recognize that it was time to awaken from the sleep of the old age and to take part in the new age already begun. Believers should respond, according to Paul, by tossing aside any works of darkness and girding themselves (for battle) with light (like a *Star Wars* light saber), transformation.

Thus light would destroy darkness, because "God has destined us
. . . for obtaining salvation through our Lord Jesus Christ, who
died for us, so that whether we are awake or asleep we may live
with him" (1 Thess 5:9–10, NRSVue).

Meditation/Journal: Are you waiting for Jesus Anointed to return? Explain. What light do you wield?

Psalm Response: "I look up to the mountains; / does my strength
come from mountains? / No, my strength comes from GOD, /
who made heaven, and earth, and mountains. / He won't let you
stumble, / your Guardian God won't fall asleep. / Not on your life!
. . . . [Your] / Guardian will never doze or sleep. / GOD's your
Guardian, / right at your side to protect you— / Shielding you
from sunstroke, / sheltering you from moonstroke. / GOD guards
you from every evil, / he guards your very life. / He guards you
when you leave and when you return, / he guards you now, he
guards you always." (Ps 121:1–8, TM)

LIFE AND DEATH

Scripture: . . . [W]e do not live to ourselves, and we do not die to
ourselves. If we live, we live to the Lord, and if we die, we die to
the Lord; so then, whether we live or whether we die, we are the
Lord's. For to this end Christ died and lived again, so that he might
be Lord of both the dead and the living." (Rom 14:7–9, NRSVue)

Reflection: The passage above highlights the gracious lordship of
the Anointed over the living and the dead. Paul has in mind the
dying to sin and the old self that took place in baptism and the
new life those who had been baptized into the Anointed's death
and resurrection received in relation to God. In his Second Letter
to the Corinthians, Paul writes: ". . . [Christ] died for all, so that
those who live might live no longer for themselves but for the one
who for their sake died and was raised" (2 Cor 5:15, NRSVue). A
baptized person's life is no longer his or her own; it belongs to God.
That is why the Anointed died and lived again; he is master of both
the dead and the living. All are encompassed by the lordship of the
Anointed; salvation is universal.

Meditation/Journal: What is your response to Paul's words about belonging to God through the lordship of Jesus Anointed?

Psalm Response: "Keep me safe, O God, / I've run for dear life to you. / I say to GOD, 'Be my Lord!' / Without you, nothing makes sense. / All these God-chosen lives all around— / what splendid friends they make! / My choice is you, GOD, first and only. / And now I find I'm *your* choice! / I'm happy from the inside out, / and from the outside in, I'm firmly formed. / Now you've got my feet on the life path, / all radiant from the shining of your face. / Ever since you took my hand, / I'm on the right way." (Ps 16:1–3, 5, 9, 11, TM)

St. Romans
P <u>1 Corinthians</u>
2 Corinthians
A Galatians
U Philippians
1 Thessalonians
1 Philemon

2

First Corinthians

CROSS

Scripture: "... [T]he message about the cross is foolishness to those who are perishing, but to us who are being saved it is the power of God. Has not God made foolish the wisdom of the world? For since, in the wisdom of God, the world did not know God through wisdom, God decided through the foolishness of the proclamation to save those who believe. For Jews ask for signs and Greeks desire wisdom, but we proclaim Christ crucified, a stumbling block to Jews and foolishness to gentiles, but to those who are the called, both Jews and Greeks, Christ the power of God and the wisdom of God. For God's foolishness is wiser than human wisdom, and God's weakness is stronger than human strength." (1 Cor 1:18, 20d–25 NRSVue)

Reflection: Paul's principle theology in Romans is justification by faith; his principle theology in his First Letter to the Corinthians concerns the cross, the act of salvation delivered to people through Paul's preaching. To non-believers, Paul's word about the cross is foolishness; it makes no sense that the savior of the world would die on the Roman instrument of capital punishment! However, to believers the cross represents the power of God; it is a paradox. The wisdom to recognize the truth of the paradox is not worldly knowledge or information; it is the ability of insight, of discernment as to how God works. Wisdom reveals the power of God. The fellow Jews to whom Paul preaches want to see signs that validate the apostle's words. The Greeks (Gentiles) to whom Paul preaches want deep wisdom (insight). According to Paul, both Jews and Greeks want God to submit himself to their criteria to believe. According to Paul, the Anointed crucified on the cross paradoxically reveals the power and the wisdom of God. Preaching a crucified Anointed is foolishness, but to God it is wisdom—a wisdom wiser than human wisdom. Preaching a crucified Anointed is weakness, but to God it is strength—a strength stronger than human strength. From a human point of view, God's wisdom appears to be foolishness in the eyes of the world. However, from God's perspective, according to Paul, it puts the wisdom of the world to shame! In his Letter to the Galatians, he writes: "May I never boast of anything except the cross of our Lord Jesus Christ, by which the world has been crucified to me and I to the world" (Gal 6:14, NRSVue). While he forbad boasting in his Letter to the Romans, he permits it in his Letter to the Galatians, albeit with his own definition of boasting. Paul declares that since salvation was not achieved through his own efforts but through the Anointed's death and resurrection, boasting is a form of glorification of the cross. "Let the one who boasts, boast in the Lord" (1 Cor 1:31, NRSVue). Thus, such boasting in the Lord is not boasting at all. By boasting in the cross, it is not Paul's boasting; it is what happened to Paul through the Anointed and his cross.

Meditation/Journal: About what do you boast? Explain. What is your spiritual foolishness? Explain.

Psalm Response: "I bless GOD every chance I get; / my lungs expand with his praise. / I live and breathe GOD; / if things aren't going well, hear this and be happy: / Join me in spreading the news; / together let's get the word out. / GOD met me more than halfway, / he freed me from my anxious fears. / When I was desperate, I called out, / and GOD got me out of a tight spot. / Open your mouth and taste, open your eyes and see— / how good GOD is. / Blessed are you who run to him." (Ps 34:1–4, 6, 8, TM)

WISDOM

Scripture: ". . . Christ did not send me to baptize but to proclaim the gospel—and not with eloquent wisdom, so that the cross of Christ might not be emptied of its power. . . . God chose what is foolish in the world to shame the wise; God chose what is weak in the world to shame the strong; God chose what is low and despised in the world, things that are not, to abolish things that are, so that no one might boast in the presence of God. . . . [W]e speak God's wisdom, a hidden mystery, which God decreed before the ages for our glory . . . . (1 Cor 1:17, 27–29; 2:7, NRSVue)

Reflection: Paul's commission is to preach the gospel, and that preaching cannot be separated from its content—the cross—and it cannot overshadow the cross to empty it of its power. The cross is foolishness in the world, but it is divine foolishness that shames the wise; it overthrows the lofty and exalts the lowly. God doesn't color within the lines that humans draw. In other words, God colors outside of human lines. God chooses the worldly weak to shame the worldly strong; God chooses what is worldly low and despised—like the cross—to achieve his purpose. Because God knows about things that have not yet come into existence, he uses them to abolish things that already exist. Thus, no one can boast in God's presence; all one can do is boast of what God did through the cross of the Anointed. That is Paul's understanding of God's wisdom; it is a hidden mystery—partially disclosed in the cross of the Anointed—which the all-knowing God decreed before time began for glorying in the cross (Gal 6:14).

Meditation/Journal: What wisdom (hidden mystery) has God given to you? How was it disclosed to you? Explain.

Psalm Response: "Listen, everyone, listen— / earth-dwellers, don't miss this. / All you haves / and have-nots, / All together now: listen. / I set plainspoken wisdom before you, / my heart-seasoned understandings of life. / I fine-tuned my ear to the sayings of the wise, / I solve life's riddle with the help of a harp. / . . . There's no such thing as self-rescue, / pulling yourself up by your bootstraps. / The cost of rescue is beyond our means, / and even then it doesn't guarantee / Life forever, or insurance / against the Black Hole." (Ps 49:1-4, 7-9, TM)

SPIRIT

Scripture: "God has revealed to us through the Spirit, for the Spirit searches everything, even the depths of God. . . . [N]o one comprehends what is truly God's except the Spirit of God. Now we have received not the spirit of the world but the Spirit that is from God, so that we may understand the gifts bestowed on us by God. And we speak of these things in words not taught by human wisdom but taught by the Spirit, interpreting spiritual things to those who are spiritual. Those who are spiritual discern all things, and they are themselves subject to no one else's scrutiny." (1 Cor 2:10, 11b-13, 15, NRSVue)

Reflection: Paul understands that God is Spirit and has breathed the spirit (breath of life) into people (Gen 2:7). Thus, Spirit connects God and people. In Greek, the word for spirit (*pneuma*) is also the word for breath and wind. Immaterial Spirit searches everything, because it is the life force (breath) in everything, even the innermost depths of God himself. Only the Spirit knows who God is. However, God has shared his Spirit with people; this is not the spirit of the world, but the divine spirit. With that connection of Spirit-spirit, God reveals himself and the gifts (graces) he shares with people to people. Paul, himself a pneumatic—one wise in the spirit or spirituality—speaks and writes and interprets the wisdom (spirit) of God to his readers, who are spiritual. That enables them to discern salvation, the things of God. Because of this life-line from God to people—spirituality—pneumatics understand revelation.

Meditation/Journal: How do you conceive of your spirituality? What image or metaphor do you use as a comparison?

Psalm Response: "Create in me a clean heart, O God, / and put a new and right spirit within me. / Do not cast me away from your presence, / and do not take your holy spirit from me. / Restore to me the joy of your salvation, / and sustain in me a willing spirit. The sacrifice acceptable to God is a broken spirit; / a broken and contrite heart, O God, you will not despise." (Ps 51:10–12, 17, NRSVue)

BUILDING

Scripture: "According to the grace of God given to me, like a wise master builder I laid a foundation, and someone else is building on it. Do you not know that you are God's temple and that God's Spirit dwells in you? (1 Cor 3:10a, 16, NRSVue)

Reflection: At first glance, the reader of the above passage may conclude that Paul is employing a construction metaphor. However, he is writing about the basics of belief. His ministry to the Corinthians is because of God's abundant grace. Living, working, and preaching in that divine gift, Paul is able to claim that he prepared the Corinthians with the basics, and co-workers are continuing. He reminds his readers that together they form a building—a temple—in which dwells God's Spirit. Later in First Corinthians, he asks: ". . . [D]o you not know that your body is a temple of the Holy Spirit within you, which you have from God and that you are not your own?" (1 Cor 6:19, NRSVue) While each individual is a dwelling place for the Spirit, it is the community of believers who form the temple, and each has gifts that belong to others in the community. Also, in his Second Letter to the Corinthians, he states, ". . . [W]e are the temple of the living God . . ." (2 Cor 6:16, NRSVue). In Pauline understanding, God's Spirit and the human spirit are connected, and when all the spirits of the community are connected, God's Spirit lives in each person and in the whole community. In other words, while there is an individual spirituality, there is also simultaneously a community spirituality.

Meditation/Journal: Is your spirituality more individualistic or more communistic? What balance do you need to put in place? Or what keeps your individual and communal spirituality balanced?

Psalm Response: "What a beautiful home, GOD-of-the-Angel-Armies! / I've always longed to live in a place like this, / Always dreamed of a room in your house, / where I could sing for joy to God alive! / And how blessed all those in whom you live, / whose lives become roads you travel; / They wind through lonesome valleys, come upon brooks, / discover cool springs and pools brimming with rain! / God-traveled, these roads curve up the mountain, and / at the last turn—. . . God in full view!" (Ps 84:1–2, 5–7, TM)

DOUGH

Scripture: "Your boasting is not a good thing. Do you not know that a little yeast leavens all of the dough? Clean out the old yeast so that you may be a new batch of dough, as you really are unleavened. For our paschal lamb, Christ, has been sacrificed. Therefore, let us celebrate the festival, not with the old yeast, the yeast of malice and evil, but with the unleavened bread of sincerity and truth." (1 Cor 5:6–8, NRSVue)

Reflection: Paul has received reports of members of the Corinthian community boasting, actively self-glorifying themselves—some type of arrogance (1 Cor 4:18). As far as the apostle is concerned, no boasting is every permitted, but whatever has been achieved is due to God's grace. To emphasize his point, Paul employs a proverb about leaven; most English translations change leaven to yeast, because yeast is understandable to modern readers. In Paul's world, leaven was a sign of impurity; before celebrating Passover, leaven was removed from the home scrupulously, so that nothing unclean or polluting could get in the way of celebrating the holy day of Passover, which, before the Jerusalem Temple was destroyed, began with the sacrifice of the Passover lambs and the pouring of their blood on the altar before sunset (the Jewish day began at sunset on the day before). Because Paul is discussing sexual immorality in the Corinthian community, he urges his readers to be like unleavened bread: holy, pure, undefiled, not polluted. Then, they will be like a new batch of dough! He compares the crucified Anointed to the slaughtered Passover lamb, a sacrifice. The community, according to Paul, is the new people of the covenant, like the people of the previous covenant, who slaughtered lambs and put their blood on the doorposts and lintels of their homes to escape the death of the firstborn. Therefore, it is time to celebrate, not with the old leaven—malice and evil—but with the unleavened bread (as Passover was marked) of sincerity and truth as followers of the Anointed. In other words, a new unleavened dough (community) has been brought into existence by God through the Anointed's blood.

Meditation/Journal: Other than yeast, what modern metaphor might Paul employ today to make his point about a new community brought into existence by God?

Psalm Response: "After Israel left Egypt, / . . . Sea took one look and ran the other way; / The mountains turned playful and skipped like rams, / the hills frolicked like spring lambs. / What's wrong with you, Sea, that you ran away? / And mountains, why did you skip like rams? / and you, hills, frolic like spring lambs? / Tremble, Earth! You're in the Lord's presence!" (Ps 114:1a, 3a, 4–5a, 6–7a, TM)

LIVE LIFE

Scripture: ". . . [L]et each of you lead the life that the Lord has assigned, to which God called you. This is my rule in all the churches. Was anyone at the time of his call already circumcised? Let him not seek to remove the mark of circumcision. Was anyone at the time of his call uncircumcised? Let him not seek circumcision. Circumcision is nothing, and uncircumcision is nothing, but obeying the commandments of God is everything. Let each of you remain in the condition in which you were called." (1 Cor 7:17–20, NRSVue)

Reflection: Because all is grace in Pauline thought, God calls people just as they are and gives them a life to lead. Paul insists that one does not have to achieve something in order to be saved; salvation (righteousness) is pure, divine gift. Furthermore, no change of status is required. The point of Paul's rule is the liberation of the individual from having to make a change of status, to do something to insure salvation. Thus, if one were Jewish when God called—circumcised—nothing is to be done. If one were Gentile when God called—uncircumcised—nothing is to be done. There existed some Jewish-Christians who thought that the circumcision of Gentiles was required; in other words, before one could be a follower of Jesus Anointed, who was Jewish, Gentiles (uncircumcised) had to become Jews (circumcised) first. Indirectly, Paul nullifies that perspective. Both circumcision and uncircumcision are nothing; such standing in the community cannot count, because the call to salvation is God's free gift offered to all! What really matters has nothing to do with who is circumcised and who is not; what matters is living the life to which God calls one. In terms of obeying the commandments of God, loving God and the neighbor applies equally to everyone. Thus, each person in the community should remain in the state in the world he was when he was called. In other words, there is no status in the community of the Anointed.

Meditation/Journal: Contrast Paul's perspective with that of the world in which you live? What do you discover?

Psalm Response: "I'm determined to watch steps and tongue / so they won't land me in trouble . . . . / 'Mum's the word,' I said, and kept quiet. / But the longer I kept silence / The worse it got— / my insides got hotter and hotter. / My thoughts boiled over; / I spilled my guts. / Tell me, what's going on, GOD? / How long do I have to live? / Oh! We're all puffs of air / Oh! We're all shadows in a campfire. / Oh! We're just spit in the wind. / We made our pile, and then we leave it. / 'What am I doing in the meantime, Lord? /

Hoping, that's what I'm doing—hoping / You'll save me . . . .'" (Ps 39:1a, 2–4a, 5b–7, TM)

THE LORD'S SUPPER

Scripture: ". . . I received from the Lord what I also handed on to you, that the Lord Jesus on the night when he was betrayed took a loaf of bread, and when he had given thanks, he broke it and said, 'This is my body that is for you. Do this in remembrance of me.' In the same way he took the cup also, after supper, saying, 'This cup is the new covenant in my blood. Do this as often as you drink it, in remembrance of me.' For as often as you eat this bread and drink the cup, you proclaim the Lord's death until he comes." (1 Cor 11:23–26, NRSVue)

Reflection: Other than the three accounts of the Lord's Supper found in the synoptic gospels (Mark 14:22––25; Matt 26:26:–29; Luke 22:17–20), the only other account is found in Paul's First Letter to the Corinthians above where he claims that the tradition he has received comes from the Lord himself without any explanation. He considers himself to be a link in the chain of the handing on from one person to another. While the tradition Paul presents is not situated within the Passover meal (as is the synoptic tradition), it, nevertheless, contains hints of a Passover meal; it is not bread and wine, but bread and cup. The formula is one of remembrance of the new covenant; in the synoptic gospels only Luke presents a new covenant; Mark and Matthew understand the shedding of Jesus' blood to be in line with the blood of the covenant sealed at Mount Horeb (Sinai). To the tradition he had received, Paul adds his own interpretation, namely, eating the bread and drinking the cup proclaim the death of the Anointed until he returns. The reader must remember that Paul expected to see the day when the Anointed returned. Thus, the Lord's Supper for Paul is a way to remember Jesus' death (and resurrection) until he returns (Parousia).

Meditation/Journal: What is your personal understanding of the meaning of the Lord's Supper? How does it compare with Paul's?

Psalm Response: "Listen, dear friends, to God's truth, / bend your ears to what I tell you. / I'm chewing on the morsel of a proverb; / I'll let you in on the sweet old truths, / Stories we heard from our fathers, / counsel we learned at our mother's knee. / We're not keeping this to ourselves, / we're passing it along to the next generation— / GOD's fame and fortune, / the marvelous things he has done. / [The Israelites] whined like spoiled children, 'Why can't God give us a decent meal in this desert? / . . . [H]ow about some fresh-baked bread?' / He rained down showers of manna to eat, / he gave them the Bread of Heaven. / They ate the bread of the mighty angels; / he sent them all the food they could eat." (Ps 78:1–4, 19, 20b, 24–25, TM)

SPIRITUAL GIFTS

Scripture: "Now concerning spiritual gifts, . . . I do not want you to be ignorant. . . . I want you to understand that no one speaking by the Spirit of God ever says, 'Let Jesus be cursed!' and no one can say, 'Jesus is Lord' except by the Holy Spirit. Now there are varieties of gifts but the same Spirit, and there are varieties of services but the same Lord, and there are varieties of activities, but it is the same God who activates all them in everyone. To each is given the manifestation of the Spirit for the common good. All these [gifts] are activated by one and the same Spirit, who allots to each one individually just as the Spirit chooses."(1 Cor 12:1, 3–7, 11, NRSVue)

Reflection: In the verses above, Paul presents his reflections on spiritual gifts, which are given by the Spirit to people in the community for the common good. For Paul, the Spirit is a supernatural power that gives rise to non-normal effects. In his Second Letter to the Corinthians, he explains, "Now the Lord is the Spirit, and where the Spirit of the Lord is, there is freedom" (2 Cor 3:17). Thus, the Spirit of the Lord cannot contradict himself by saying, "Let Jesus be cursed!" When one says, "Jesus is Lord," he or she is doing so because of the prompting of the Holy Spirit. Spiritual gifts— utterances of wisdom, utterances of knowledge, faith, healing, deeds, prophecy, discernment of spirits, tongues, interpretation of tongues (1 Cor 12:8–10)—are phenomena of the Spirit; they are gifts of grace, acts of service, and operations. They are given to people in the community for upbuilding; the freely given gift is not for personal ownership; it is given to be given away; in the individual it is a manifestation of the Spirit given freely by the Spirit with the purpose of being used for the common good of the community. In a me-first culture that owns its gifts and uses them to make a lot of money Paul's reflection may be difficult to hear.

Meditation/Journal: What are your spiritual gifts? In what specific ways do you use each for the common good?

Psalm Response: "What a wildly wonderful world, GOD! / You made it all, with Wisdom at your side, / made earth overflow with your wonderful creations. / All the creatures look expectantly to you / to give them their meals on time. / You come, and they gather around; / you open your hand and they eat from it. / If you turned your back, / they'd die in a minute— / Take back your Spirit and they die, / revert to original mud; / Send out your Spirit and they spring to life— / the whole countryside in bloom and blossom. / The glory of GOD— / let it last forever! / Let GOD enjoy his creation!" (Ps 104:24, 27–31, TM)

LOVE

Scripture: "Love is patient; love is kind; love is not envious or boastful or arrogant or rude. It does not insist on its own way; it is not irritable; it keeps no record of wrongs; it does not rejoice in wrongdoing but rejoices in the truth. It bears all things, believes all things, hopes all things, endures all thing. Love never ends." (1 Cor 13:4–8a, NRSVue)

Reflection: The Greek word translated into English as love is *agape*, self-sacrificial love. It is the word Paul uses in the passage above. While English has but one word for love, Greek has four words for love: *agape*, God's self-sacrificing nature; *philia*, brotherly or sisterly affectionate love between equals; *storge*, natural affection between husband and wife or between parents and children; and *eros*, sexual passion, emotional involvement, intimate or romantic love. For Paul, *agape* is a believer's concept, best described by personification. The way of love involves long suffering and the demonstration of kindness. In one who loves (*agape*), there is no envy, boast, arrogance, rudeness, getting one's own way, irritability, or keeping a record of wrongs. *Agape* love rejoices in truth—the truth of the gospel—while it bears all things, believes all things, hopes all things, and endures all things. That is why self-sacrificial love never fails or ends; it is a participation in divine love.

Meditation/Journal: On the top of a sheet of paper in four columns write *agape, philia, storge,* and *eros*. Under each word for love write the names of people you love in that way. When finished, ask yourself: What do I learn about myself from this exercise?

Psalm Response: "Show me how you work, GOD; / School me in your ways. / Take me by the hand; / Lead me down the path of truth. / You are my Savior, aren't you? / Mark the milestones of your mercy and love, GOD; / Mark me with your sign of love. / Plan only the best for me, GOD! / From now on every road you travel / Will take you to GOD." (Ps 25:4–6a, 7b, 10a, TM)

GOSPEL

Scripture: Now I want you to understand . . . the good news that I proclaimed to you, which you in turn received, in which also you stand, through which also you are being saved, if you hold firmly to the message that I proclaimed to you . . . . Christ died for our sins in accordance with the scriptures and that he was buried and that he was raised on the third day in accordance with the scriptures . . . ." (1 Cor 15:1–2, 3b–5, NRSVue)

Reflection: The Greek word *euangelion* can be translated into English as *gospel* or *good news*. When hearing the word gospel, some people think of the four gospels (Mark, Matthew, Luke, John) found in the New Testament. For Paul, gospel means that Jesus died, was buried, and was raised. The passage above begins chapter 15 of Paul's First Letter to the Corinthians; all of chapter 15 is a treatise on the resurrection of the dead. In other words, Paul is going to present his proclamation—sometimes referred to as his creed—which he has received and which the Corinthians now stand or have received. These are saving words about a saving event; Jesus Anointed died, was buried, was raised, and appeared to some people. When he writes about the Anointed dying for sins, he most likely has in mind the prophet Isaiah's words about a suffering servant: ". . . [H]e has borne our infirmities / and carried our diseases, / yet we accounted him stricken, / struck down by God, and afflicted. / But he was wounded for our transgressions, / crushed for our iniquities; / upon him was the punishment that makes us whole, / and by his bruises we are healed" (Isa 53:4–5, NRSVue). It is important to note that Paul says nothing about an empty tomb, like the four gospels do. Paul's emphasis is on the Anointed's death and burial; his being raised on the third day is a then-standard way of expressing the resurrection based on words written by the prophet Hosea: "After two days [the LORD] will revive us; / on the third day he will raise us up, / that we may live before him" (Hos 6:2, NRSVue). Also missing is Paul's usual reference to the Parousia, the Anointed's second coming.

Meditation/Journal: What do you consider to be the most important word or phrase in Paul's creed? Explain.

Psalm Response: "GOD, you're my last chance of the day. / I spent the night on my knees before you. / Put me on your salvation agenda . . . . / I'm written off as a lost cause, / one more statistic, a hopeless case. / Abandoned as already dead, / one more body in a stack of corpses, / And not so much as a gravestone— / I'm a black hole in oblivion. / Are the dead a live audience for your miracles? / Do ghosts every join the choirs that praise you? / Does your love make any difference in a graveyard? / . . . Are your marvelous wonders ever seen in the dark, / your righteous ways noticed in the Land of No memory?" (Ps 88:1–2, 5–6, 10–12, TM)

LEAST

Scripture: ". . . I am the least of the apostles, unfit to be called an apostle, because I persecuted the church of God. But by the grace of God I am what I am, and his grace toward me has not been in vain." (1 Cor 15:9–10a, NRSVue)

Reflection: In his Letter to the Galatians, Paul expresses his un-worthiness at being called an apostle in the same way as he does in his First Letter to the Corinthians. He writes, "You have heard, no doubt, of my earlier life in Judaism. I was violently persecuting the church of God and was trying to destroy it" (Gal 1:13). Paul considers grace, a free gift from God, to be the absolute factor that promoted him to apostleship. In other words, apostleship is not due to his own credit. He is what he is—an apostle—because of God's grace, which has not been in vain because Paul has been preaching the gospel; he has been doing what God called him to do. His achievement is not due to his own motivation; it is the grace of God that has moved him to act. In his Letter to the Philip-pians, he lists his credentials, which in the light of grace, mean nothing: "If anyone else has reason to be confident in the flesh, I have more: circumcised on the eighth day, a member of the people of Israel, of the tribe of Benjamin, a Hebrew born of Hebrews; as to the law, a Pharisee; as to zeal, a persecutor of the church; to the righteousness under the law, blameless" (Phil 3:4b–6). Then, he adds, "Yet whatever gains I had, these I have come to regard as loss because of Christ" (Phil 3:7). God has overwhelmed Paul with himself (grace) who works through Paul to accomplish what God wills.

Meditation/Journal: What specific ways has God motivated your life with grace?

Psalm Response: "My heart bursts its banks, / spilling beauty and goodness. / I pour it out in a poem . . . , / shaping the river into words: / 'You're the handsomest of men; / every word from your lips is sheer grace, / and God has blessed you, blessed you so much. / Ride majestically! Ride triumphantly! / Ride on the side of truth! / Ride for the righteous meek! / I'll make you famous for genera-tions; / you'll be the talk of the town / for a long, long time.'" Ps 45:1–2, 4, 17, TM)

RESURRECTION

Scripture: ". . . [I]f Christ is proclaimed as raised from the dead, how can some of you say there is no resurrection of the dead? If there is no resurrection of the dead, then Christ has not been raised, and if Christ has not been raised, then our proclamation is in vain and your faith is in vain. . . . [If] the dead are not raised, then Christ has not been raised. If Christ has not been raised, your faith is futile, and you are still in your sins. But in fact Christ has been raised from the dead, the first fruits of those who have died. For since death came through a human, the resurrection of the dead has also come through a human, for as all die in Adam, so all will be made alive in Christ." (1 Cor 15:12–14, 16–17, 20–22, NRSVue)

Reflection: Paul presupposes the resurrection of the Anointed; it has been a part of his gospel (proclamation). However, in Corinth (as elsewhere), there are those declaring that there is no such thing as resurrection of the dead. In common experience, the dead tend to stay dead! Paul refuses to isolate the faith-event; it is part of the total gospel: the Anointed died, was buried, and was raised. If it is not believed, then faith becomes futility; people have not been set free from their sins; they have not been justified in the Anointed, if he has not been raised. According to Paul, the Anointed has been raised; he is the first to experience resurrection from the dead, but there are more to come. In the mythology of the Hebrew Bible (Old Testament), Adam is considered the primal man, that is, the one in whom all people are contained. Thus, death for all proceeds from him, since all humanity is contained in him. Paul reshapes that mythology; all who are in the Anointed have been transformed. If Adam brought the transformation from life to death, the Anointed brought the transformation from death to life; that transformation is named resurrection, and the Anointed was the first to experience it.

Meditation/Journal: How do you picture, describe, think about, talk about resurrection? What do you think resurrection is?

Canticle Response: "Think of yourselves the way Christ Jesus thought of himself. He had equal status with God but didn't think so much of himself that he had to cling to the advantages of that status no matter what. Not at all. When the time came, he set aside the privileges of deity and took on the status of a slave, became *human*! Having become human, he stayed human. It was an incredibly humbling process. He didn't claim special privileges. Instead, he lived a selfless, obedient life and then died a selfless, obedient death—and the worst kind of death at that—a crucifixion. Because of that obedience, God lifted him high and honored him far beyond anyone or anything, ever, so that all created beings in heaven and on earth—even those long ago dead and buried—will bow in worship before this Jesus Christ, and call out in praise that he is the Master of all, to the glorious honor of God the Father" (Phil 2:5–11, TM)

BODILY RESURRECTION

Scripture: ". . . [S]omeone will ask, 'How are the dead raised? With what kind of body do they come?' Fool! What you sow does not come to life unless it dies. And as for what you sow, you do not sow the body that is to be but a bare seed . . . . But God gives it a body as he has chosen and to each kind of seed its own body. So it is with the resurrection of the dead. What is sown is perishable; what is raised is imperishable. It is sown a physical body; it is raised a spiritual body. If there is a physical body, there is also a spiritual body. (1 Cor 15:35–38, 42, 44, NRSVue)

Reflection: Even though there are two questions Paul presents, the first is set aside, while the second is addressed. It is clear that Paul cannot conceive of existence without a body. However, because he has not died and been raised, he cannot know what a resurrected body is! So, he proposes an analogy using the metaphor of a seed. A seed has a body, but what is planted is not the body it has when it sprouts and grows. Death transforms a seed from one body to another. The emphasis is on the life of the body after the seed dies. In Pauline understanding, after the human body dies, God makes it imperishable; it is no longer physical, but spiritual. Death is necessary for the transformation of the seed to a plant and for the transformation from a physical body to a spiritual body for a person. What was put into the earth is not what rises out of the earth. God creates anew. Paul calls it a spiritual body or a body of spirit. Paul thinks of it as a spirit substance, no matter how impossible it is to conceive of something not physical as substance!

Meditation/Journal: What do you think a spiritual body is? Explain.

Psalm Response: "Not for our sake, GOD, no, not for our sake, / but for your name's sake show your glory. / Do it on account of your merciful love, / do it on account of your faithful ways. / Our God is in heaven / doing whatever he wants to do. / . . . [P]ut your trust in GOD! / —trust your Helper! Trust your Ruler! / May you be blessed by GOD, / by GOD, who made heaven and earth. / Dead people can't praise GOD— / not a word to be heard from those buried in the ground. / But we bless GOD, oh yes— / we bless him now, we bless him always! / Hallelujah!" (Ps 115:1, 3, 9, 15, 17–18, TM)

TRANSFORMED

Scripture: "We will not all die, but we will all be changed, in a moment, in the twinkling of an eye, at the last trumpet. For the trumpet will sound, and the dead will be raised imperishable, and we will be changed." (1 Cor 15:51b–52, NRSVue)

Reflection: The passage above confirms Paul's belief that he would be alive when the Anointed returned (Parousia). He expressed the same idea in his First Letter to the Thessalonians: ". . . [W]e declare to you by the word of the Lord, that we who are alive, who are left until the coming of the Lord, will by no means precede those who have died. For the Lord himself, with a cry of command, with the archangel's call and with the sound of God's trumpet, will descend from heaven, and the dead in Christ will rise first. Then we who are alive, who are left, will be caught up in the clouds together with them to meet the Lord in the air, and so we will be with the Lord forever" (1 Thess 4:15–17, NRSVue). Paul thinks that the end will come instantly. Suddenly, in the time it takes to blink the eyes, the (God's) trumpet heralding the end will be heard, and all who have died believing in the Anointed will be transformed into whatever a risen or glorified body is! While these words were meant to be encouragement to the readers (1 Thess 4:18), time passed, Paul died, and the Parousia never occurred. In other words, Paul was wrong. For whatever transformation Paul hoped to experience, two thousand years later it remains in the future.

Meditation/Journal: What transformation do you think will take place after death? after the Parousia?

Psalm Response: "Applause, everyone. Bravo, bravissimo! / Shout God-songs at the top of your lungs! / GOD Most High is stunning . . . . / Loud cheers as God climbs the mountain, / a ram's horn blast at the summit. / Sing songs to God, sing out! / Sing to our King, sing praise! / He's Lord over earth, / so sing your best songs to God. / The powers of earth are God's— / he soars over all." (Ps 47:1–2, 5–7, 9b, TM)

WRITE

Scripture: "I, Paul, write this greeting with my own hand." (1 Cor 16:21, NRSVue)

Reflection: Paul's statement at the end of his First Letter to the Corinthians implies that there was a secretary either writing or copying the letter. In his letter to the Galatians, he writes, "See what large letters I make when I am writing in my own hand!" (Gal 6:11) Also, in his letter to Philemon, he writes, "I, Paul, am writing this with my own hand" (Phlm 1:19a). Because the apostle used this technique in what are considered to be his genuine letters, authors of second-generation letters adopted its use to convince readers and "authenticate" their writings for a new generation of believers (Col 4:18; 2 Thess 3:17). Just as Paul wishes to underscore the importance of what he writes in his letters, the use of the form in second generation Pauline letters serves to authenticate the letter. Such use is comparable to the use of italics, capitalization, bold, and underlining available to writers using computer word processing programs today.

Meditation/Journal: What do you consider today to be like Paul's words about writing a part of the letter (greeting) with his own hand?

Canticle Response: "Write what you see. / Write it out in big block letters / so that it can be read on the run. / The vision-message is a witness / pointing to what's coming. / It aches for the coming—it can hardly wait! / And it doesn't lie. / If it seems slow in coming, wait. / It's on its way. It will come right on time." (Hab 2:2b–3, TM)

3

Second Corinthians

AROMA

Scripture: ". . . [W]e are the aroma of Christ to God among those who are being saved and among those who are perishing: to the one group a fragrance from death to death, to the other a fragrance from life to life." (2 Cor 2:15–16a, NRSVue)

Reflection: After the usual Pauline introduction in his Second Letter to the Corinthians, Paul introduces the metaphor of the fragrance that comes from knowing the Anointed (2 Cor 2:14). The only other place in the original Pauline collection of letters where he employs the olfactory metaphor is in his Letter to the Philippians, where he refers to gifts he has received as "a fragrant offering, a sacrifice acceptable and pleasing to God" (Phil 4:18). In the passage above he does not have in mind a burnt offering; rather, he employs the metaphor of smell. Paul uses the words—*aroma* and *fragrance*—in both a positive and a negative sense. Aroma connotes a pleasant (positive) smell. Thus, according to Paul, believers (especially Corinthian believers) are the pleasant smell of Christ to God among both those being saved and those who are perishing. It is like driving on a road and having a pleasant smell enter all the cars passing through it; everyone gets a whiff of the aroma. However, according to Paul, for those who believe in what God did in the Anointed, it is a fragrance that enhances life. For those who do not believe, it is a fragrance that smells like death. Paul thinks that both life (salvation) and death (perdition) are already being achieved (lived) now, because it is God who directs all things.

Meditation/Journal: In what specific ways are you an aroma of Christ to God? Are you a fragrance, a whiff, odor, perfume, etc.? Explain.

Canticle Response: "All people of God, bless the Lord; praise and honor him forever. / Souls of the just, bless the Lord; praise and honor him forever. / All who are holy and humble of heart, bless the Lord; praise and honor him forever. / Stand up and proclaim the greatness of the Lord; he is goodness itself and his mercy never quits. / All who are in awe of the God of gods, bless the Lord; stand up and proclaim him, for his mercy never quits." (Dan 3:85–87, 89–90, TM)

LETTERS

Scripture: "Surely we do not need, as some do, letters of recommendation to you or from you, do we? You yourselves are our letter, written on our hearts, known and read by all, and you show that you are a letter of Christ, prepared by us, written not with ink but with the Spirit of the living God, not on tablets of stone but on tablets that are human hearts. [God] has made us qualified to be ministers of a new covenant, not of letter but of spirit, for the letter kills, but the Spirit gives life." (2 Cor 3:1b–3, 6, NRSVue)

Reflection: In Paul's time, letters of introduction and recommendation were used throughout the world to establish one's credentials.

Paul uses that metaphor in his Second Letter to the Corinthians in several ways. First, his opening question to his Corinthians readers solicits a negative response: Because he has written to them before, they do not need a letter or recommendation. Second, he tells them that they collectively are a letter written on Paul's heart, the very core of a person where God's Spirit is active. They are read by all through the way they live their lives. Third, the Corinthians are also a letter of the Anointed; this means that the Corinthians collectively formed the body of Christ. Thus, the Anointed is operative in Paul's work in the community. The letter of the Anointed was written by Paul, like a secretary or scribe would write a letter. Fourth, the Corinthian letter was not written with ink, as most letters were, but with the Spirit of the living God. Just like ink leaves a mark on paper, God has left his invisible mark with Spirit on the hearts of believers. In Pauline thought, it is God's Spirit that connects to people's spirit, like the electrical line from the pole outside the house connects to the switches and plugs inside the house to supply electricity. Fifth, just to make sure the Corinthians understand, Paul tells them that they are not like the previous covenant of Torah chiseled into stone tablets (Exod 24:12; 31:18; 34:1; Deut 9:10–11); the Spirit writes a new covenant on human hearts (Jer 31:31–34). And Paul considers himself a minister of the new covenant, not of Torah, which kills, but of Spirit, which gives life. Ironically, for Paul, trained to be a Pharisee who keeps Torah, he preaches the end of Torah and the time of the life-giving Spirit.

Meditation/Journal: In what specific ways are you a letter written in Spirit by God?

Psalm Response: "Hallelujah! / I give thanks to GOD with everything I've got— / Wherever good people gather, and in the congregation. / GOD's works are so great, worth / A lifetime of study—endless enjoyment! / Splendor and beauty mark his craft; / His generosity never gives out. / His miracles are his memorial— / This GOD of Grace, this GOD of Love. / He ordered his Covenant kept forever. / He's so personal and holy, worthy of our respect. / The good life begins in the fear of GOD— / Do that and you'll know the blessing of GOD. / His Hallelujah lasts forever!" (Ps 111:1–4, 9–10, TM)

NEW COVENANT

Scripture: ". . . [W]hen one turns to the Lord, the veil is removed. Now the Lord is the Spirit, and where the Spirit of the Lord is, there is freedom. And all of us, with unveiled faces seeing the glory of the Lord as though reflected in a mirror, are being transformed into the same image from one degree of glory to another, for this comes from the Lord the Spirit." (2 Cor 3:16–18, NRSVue)

Reflection: In order to understand the above passage about the veil, the reader must know the story in the Hebrew Bible (Old Testament) book of Exodus: "When Moses had finished speaking with [the Israelites], he put a veil on his face, but whenever Moses went in [the tabernacle] before the LORD to speak with him, he would take the veil off until he came out, and when he came out and told the Israelites what he had been commanded, the Israelites would see the face of Moses, that the skin of his face was shining, and Moses would put the veil on his face again until he went in to speak with him" (Exod 34:33–35, NRSVue). Paul interprets that story to refer to the first (old) covenant that was being set aside (2 Cor 3:13). According to Paul, when the Jews "hear the reading of the old covenant, the same veil is still there; it is not unveiled since in Christ it is set aside" (2 Cor 3:14, NRSVue). Then he adds, "Indeed, to this very day whenever Moses is read, a veil lies over their minds" (2 Cor 3:15, NRSVue). However, when people turn to God, the veil is removed. God, who is Spirit, has established a new covenant of Spirit to replace the old one of the letter. The Anointed, the Lord Jesus, is experienced through the Spirit, and where the Spirit is, there is freedom from the old covenant of attempting to earn salvation. The new covenant brings the free gifts of justification, life, and transformation. Thus, believers with unveiled faces see the glory of God revealed by the Anointed. It is like looking at blinding light reflected in a mirror. The transformation that happened to Moses is a possibility for every believer in the Anointed.

74

If the believer looks into a mirror, he or she does not see himself or herself; he or she sees the image of the Anointed, which manifests God's glory in degrees, and is accomplished by the Spirit.

Meditation/Journal: When you look into a mirror, whom do you see?

Psalm Response: "GOD, brilliant Lord, / yours is a household name. / I look up at your macro-skies, dark and enormous, / your handmade sky-jewelry, / Moon and stars mounted in their settings. / Then I look at my micro-self and wonder, / Why do you bother with us? / Why take a second look our way? / Yet we've so narrowly missed being gods, / bright with Eden's dawn light. / You put us in charge of your handcrafted world, / repeated to us your Genesis-charge . . . . / GOD, brilliant Lord, / your name echoes around the world." (Ps 8:1, 3–6, 9, TM)

CLAY JARS

Scripture: ". . . [W]e proclaim Jesus Christ as Lord and ourselves as your slaves for Jesus's sake. . . . [W]e have this treasure in clay jars, so that it may be made clear that this extraordinary power belongs to God and does not come from us." (2 Cor 4:5, 7, NRSVue)

Reflection: In Paul's world, a clay jar could be one that was fired (bisqueware, without glaze) or it could be what we call greenware (dried mud but not fired) today. Either way, it was very fragile. Paul metaphorically compares believers to fragile clay jars into which has been received and placed his message that the Anointed died, was buried, and was raised; Paul himself is a servant of Jesus. As he does in other letters, he makes it very clear to the Corinthians that the power of the gospel—the message Paul proclaims—does not come from him; it belongs to and comes from God. Paul is minister of the good news. Thus, all believers, including Paul, are fragile clay jars into which has been placed the gospel of God.

Meditation/Journal: In what specific ways are you like a clay jar?

Psalm Response: "I run to you, GOD; I run for dear life. / Don't let me down! / Take me seriously this time! / Be kind to me, GOD— / I'm in deep, deep trouble again. / My friends are horrified; / they cross the street to avoid me. / They want to blot me from memory, / forget me like a corpse in a grave, / discard me like a broken dish in the trash. / Desperate, I throw myself on you; / *you* are my God! / Hour by hour I place my days in your hand, / safe from the hands out to get me." (Ps 31:1, 9, 11b–12, 14–15, TM)

TENT

Scripture: ". . . [W]e know that, if the earthly tent we live in is destroyed, we have a building from God, a house not made with hands, eternal in the heavens. For while we are in this tent, we groan under our burden because we wish not to be unclothed but to be further clothed, so that what is mortal may be swallowed up by life. The one who has prepared us for this very thing is God, who has given us the Spirit as a down payment. . . . [W]hile we are at home in the body we are away from the Lord—for we walk by faith, not by sight. Yes, we do have confidence, and we would rather be away from the body and at home with the Lord." (2 Cor 5:1, 4–8, NRSVue)

Reflection: A tent is a collapsible or moveable shelter; it covers or protects the body. Paul uses tent as a metaphor for the mortal body; in other words, while on earth, we live in a tent. However, when the tent is destroyed—when the body dies, we can be confident that God has a permanent shelter (house) for us in which to live. In the meantime, while we live in a tent, we groan physically, mentally, and spiritually, because we do not wish to be unclothed in death but, rather, to be more clothed with God. In other words, we look forward to mortality being consumed by immortality. Paul is confident of this taking place because of God's gift of immortal Spirit. We experience the immortal Spirit of God through its connection to our immortal spirit. Because we are mortal, we are at home in our bodily tent, but we are way from God. While living in the tent, we walk by faith, trusting God. We trust that after we die—when we leave the body—we will enter God's house and be at home with him. It is important here not to conclude that Paul is writing about the Aristotelian body-soul dichotomy; for Paul it is a glorified body-spirit unity that continues after death, referred to as resurrection. In his Letter to the Philippians, he explains: "[The Lord Jesus Christ] will transform the body of our humiliation that it may be conformed to the body of his glory, by the power that also enables him to make all things subject to himself" (Phil 3:21, NRSVue).

Meditation/Journal: Do you live in a tent, a building, or a house? What are the consequences of your answer? Explain.

Psalm Response: "God, listen to my shout, / bend an ear to my prayer. / When I'm far from anywhere, / down to my last gasp, / I call out, 'Guide me / up High Rock Mountain.' / You've always given me breathing room, / a place to get away from it all, / A lifetime pass to your safe-house, / an open invitation as your guest. / You've always taken me seriously, God, / made me welcome among those who know and love you. / . . . [P]ost Steady Love and Good Faith as lookouts, / And I'll be the poet who sings your glory— / and live what I sing every day." (Ps 61:1–5, 8, TM)

RECONCILIATION

Scripture: ". . . [T]he love of Christ urges us on, because we are convinced that one has died for all; therefore all have died. And he died for all so that those who live might live no longer for themselves but for the one who for their sake died and was raised. So if anyone is in Christ, there is a new creation; everything old has passed away; look, new things have come into being! All this is from God, who reconciled us to himself through Christ and has given us the ministry of reconciliation; that is, in Christ God was reconciling the world to himself . . . . So we are ambassadors for Christ, since God is making his appeal through us, we entreat you on behalf of Christ: be reconciled to God. For our sake God made the one who knew no sin to be sin, so that in him we might become the righteousness of God." (2 Cor 5:14–15, 17–21, NRSVue)

Reflection: The love of the Anointed holds Paul in its grip! The reason he gives is based on his conclusion that Jesus manifested his love through his death on a cross. That self-sacrificial love urges

Paul to the service of preaching the gospel. Because Paul presents the Anointed as God's new creation, he died for all, and all have, therefore, died because they are incorporated into his body. The purpose of his death was to give an example to those who live; they should no longer live for themselves but for him in self-sacrificial love. In other words, a response is necessary once one hears the gospel about the Anointed's death and resurrection. Believers have been newly created in the Anointed. "[A] new creation is everything!" states Paul in his Letter to the Galatians (6:15, NRSVue). What was old or previous has given way to new things; this is another act of God. One aspect of the new creation is the reconciliation with God the Anointed accomplished. Through the Anointed, God reconciled humankind to himself, and he entrusted the message of that reconciliation to those, like Paul, who are ministers of the gospel. Through such ministers—ambassadors, who represent the divine—God makes known his will. Paul exhorts his readers to accept the reconciliation offered by God through the Anointed, rather than attempting to reconcile themselves to God. After all, for the sake of all humankind, God made the Anointed a human, a representative of all sinners, so that he could reconcile all to himself through him. In other words, through the Anointed, all people become righteous through the righteousness of God. The Anointed is the first of the new creation; God raised him from the dead. People do not reconcile themselves to God; God has already done that. All people can do is accept God's gift and make a response in the way they live their lives.

Meditation/Journal: In what specific ways does the love of Christ urge you to demonstrate by your lifestyle that you are reconciled to God? Explain.

Psalm Response: "Thank GOD! He deserves your thanks, / *His love never quits*. / Thank the God of all gods, / *His love never quits*. / Thank the Lord of all lords. / *His love never quits*. / God remembered us when we were down, / *His love never quits*. / Rescued us from the trampling boot, / *His love never quits*. / Takes care of everyone in time of need, / *His love never quits*. / Thank God, who did it all! / *His love never quits*." (Ps 136:1–3, 23–26, TM)

St. Romans
P 1 Corinthians
   2 Corinthians
A <u>Galatians</u>
U Philippians
   1 Thessalonians
l Philemon

4

Galatians

REVELATION OF GOD'S SON

Scripture: ". . . [W]hen the one who had set me apart before I was born and called me through his grace was pleased to reveal his Son to me, so that I might proclaim him among the gentiles, I did not confer with any human." (Gal 1:15–16, NRSVue)

Reflection: Many people are familiar with the accounts of Paul's conversion due to an appearance of the risen Anointed One in the Acts of the Apostles (9:1–22; 22:3–16; 26:12–18). However, those accounts are written by the same author who wrote Luke's Gospel. In the genuine Pauline letters, Paul makes no mention of a blinding light, hearing a voice, and being baptized. In his First Letter to the Corinthians, he states, "Last of all, as to one untimely born, [Christ] appeared also to me" (1 Cor 15:8, NRSVue). Earlier in the same letter, he had asked rhetorically his readers: "Am I not an apostle? Have I not seen Jesus our Lord?" (1 Cor 9:1bc, NRSVue) He regards everything as loss in light of the surpassing value of knowing the Anointed Jesus (Phil 3:8a). He tells the Philippians that he desires to gain Christ "and be found in him, not having a righteousness of my own that comes from the law, but one that comes through faith in Christ, the righteousness from God based on faith" (Phil 3:9, NRSVue). Because of his experience of the revelation of God's Son, he wants to be conformed through suffering, death, and resurrection to the Anointed One (Phil 3:10–11).

Meditation/Journal: In what specific ways have you experienced Jesus Anointed?

Psalm Response: "My head is high, GOD, held high; / I'm looking to you, GOD . . . . / I've thrown in my lot with you . . . . / Show me how you work, GOD; / School me in your ways. / Take me by the hand; / Lead me down the path of truth. / You are my Savior, aren't you? / Mark the milestones of your mercy and love, GOD . . . . / From now one every road you travel / Will take you to GOD, / Follow the Covenant signs; / Read the charted directions." (Ps 25:1–3a, 4–6a, 10, TM)

JUSTIFICATION

Scripture: ". . . [W]e know that a person is justified not by the works of the law but through the faith of Jesus Christ. And we have come to believe in Christ Jesus, so that we might be justified by the faith of Christ and not by doing the works of the law, because no one will be justified by the works of the law." (Gal 2:16, NRSVue)

Reflection: The above passage is a clear statement of Paul's understanding of justification by faith. If one could be justified by doing the works of Torah, then he or she could earn it. Then, what did Jesus do? By declaring that one could not achieve salvation through the works of Torah, Paul denies the basic Pharisaic Jewish doctrine of salvation. However, by denying salvation by Torah observance, he opens a wedge in which to explain what God did in and through Jesus Anointed. Justification by God is mediated by the Anointed to those who believe—who have faith—that he is the Messiah (Anointed), the Christ (Anointed). Jesus is the channel of salvation from God to people. Faith in Jesus Anointed is belief that he was crucified, buried, and raised by God. This understanding does not mean that the works of Torah do not need to be done; according to Paul, the works do not produce justification before God. Thus, according to Pauline understanding, justification is a free gift from God—that cannot be earned through works of Torah—mediated by Jesus Anointed and believed by Jews and Gentiles.

Meditation/Journal: Do you engage in good works to earn salvation? Explain. Do you accept justification through Jesus Christ and respond to the free gift with good works? Explain.

Psalm Response: "Listen to this prayer of mine, GOD; / pay attention to what I'm asking. / Answer me—you're famous for your answers! / Do what's right for me. / Hurry with your answer, GOD! / I'm nearly at the end of my rope. / Don't turn away; don't ignore me! / That would be certain death. / If you wake me each morning with the sound of your loving voice, / I'll go to sleep each night trusting in you. / Point out the road I must travel; / I'm all ears, all eyes before you." (Ps 143:1, 7–8, TM)

CHRIST ALIVE

Scripture: ". . . [T[hrough the law I died to the law, so that I might live to God. I have been crucified with Christ, and it is no longer I who live, but it is Christ who lives in me. And the life I now live in the flesh I live by the faith of the Son of God, who loved me and gave himself for me. I do not nullify the grace of God, for if righteousness comes through the law, then Christ died for nothing." (Gal 2:19–21, NRSVue)

Reflection: In the above passage from Galatians, Paul presents four statements that are worthy of reflection. The first is about dying to Torah through Torah in order to live to God. For Paul, the time of Torah has passed; people are no longer subject to Torah (Gal 3:25). In his Letter to the Romans, he writes: ". . . [Y]ou have died to the law through the body of Christ, so that you may belong to another, to him who was raised from the dead in order that we may bear fruit for God" (Rom 7:4). Dying to Torah means setting aside the attempt to earn righteousness by doing the works of Torah, and, put simply, accepting that God makes people righteous so they can live for him. Second, Paul declares that he has been crucified with the Anointed. In his Letter to the Romans, he interprets the ritual of baptism as a death and resurrection with the Anointed (Rom 6:1–10). Third, as a member of the corporate body of Christ, the Anointed lives in him and he in the Anointed. The life he lives now, as a member of the body of Christ, he lives by justification by faith in the Son of God. In other words, the Anointed lives in Paul. The resurrected Anointed is identical with the Spirit (2 Cor 3:17a), who provides life for God for him; spirit is connected to Spirit. Fourth, while Paul still lives in the flesh, he lives in the acceptance of the righteousness that comes through faith in the Anointed, who both loved him and gave himself for him through death, burial, and resurrection. While Paul is alive in the flesh (because he has not died), he is also alive in the Anointed through the Spirit. If the four statements are true, as Paul believes they are, then the process of salvation is by the grace of God. Righteousness cannot come through Torah, because, if it does, the Anointed died for nothing; the death, burial, and resurrection of the Anointed accomplished nothing, if keeping Torah can achieve the same results!

Meditation/Journal: Which one of Paul's four statements gets most of your attention? What new idea or insight does it give to you? Explain. How will you apply that new idea or insight to your life?

Psalm Response: "When I call, give me answers, God, take my side! / Once, in a tight place, you gave me room; . . . / grace me! hear me! / Look at this: look / Who got picked by GOD! / He listens the split second I call to him. / Complain if you must, but don't lash out; / Keep your mouth shut, and let your heart do the talking. / Build your case before God and wait for his verdict." (Ps 4:1, 3–5, TM)

SPIRIT

Scripture: "Did you receive the Spirit by doing the works of the law or by believing what you heard? Are you so foolish? Having started with the Spirit, are you now ending with the flesh?" (Gal 3:2b–3, NRSVue)

Reflection: In Galatia, Paul has discovered that there are Jewish-Christians, who are more Jewish than Pauline Christians, teaching that one must become a Torah-observant Jew first before believing that Jesus was the Anointed (Messiah, Christ). Torah-observance was primarily about circumcision, as we will see below. For Paul, the time for Torah has passed away; the new covenant God has initiated with his people is in the Anointed Jesus, who died, was buried, and raised by God. With this understanding, Paul refers to the Galatians as foolish and having been bewitched (Gal 3:2) or fooled. To make his point, he asks the readers of his letter if they received the Spirit by doing the works of Torah or by believing what they heard Paul preach. He is asking them to use their own experience, which contradicts their present inclination to accept Torah and circumcision. Paul expects that they will answer that they received the Spirit as a result of his preaching, whereby God sent the spirit of Jesus Anointed into their hearts and they cried, "Abba! Father!" (Gal 4:6). Because their experience of Spirit occurred outside of Torah observance, it was not the result of doing the works of the Torah. Thus, they are foolish because they are contradicting themselves. They began in the Spirit, according to Paul, and that is how they should finish. They should not fall into Torah, because it leads to circumcision of the flesh; they should continue in Spirit from which they will reap eternal life. As he writes, "If we live by the Spirit, let us also be guided by the Spirit" (Gal 5:25, NRSVue).

Meditation/Journal: Do you live more according to the Spirit or according to Torah (Law, works)? Explain.

Psalm Response: "How well God must like you— / . . . you thrill to GOD's Word, / you chew on Scripture day and night. / You're a tree replanted in Eden, / bearing fresh fruit every month, / Never dropping a leaf, / always in blossom. / GOD charts the road you take." (Ps 1:1a, 2–3, 6a, TM)

LAW

Scripture: "Why then the law? It was added because of transgressions, until the offspring would come to whom the promise had been made . . . . Is the law then opposed to the promises of God? Certainly not! For if a law had been given that could make alive, then righteousness would indeed come through the law. But the scripture has imprisoned all things under the power of sin, so that what was promised through the faith of Jesus Christ might be given to those who believe. Now before faith came, we were imprisoned and guarded under the law until faith would be revealed. . . . [N]ow that faith has come, we are no longer subject to a disciplinarian [Law], for in Christ Jesus you are all children of God through faith. As many of you as were baptized into Christ have clothed yourselves with Christ. And if you belong to Christ, then you are Abraham's offspring, heirs according to the promise." (Gal 3:19, 21–23, 25–27, 29, NRSVue)

Reflection: In the passage above from his Letter to the Galatians, Paul explains the function and purpose of Torah. While reading this portion of his letter, the reader must keep in mind that Saul (Paul) was a Torah-observant Pharisee before he experienced Jesus Anointed. Torah, considered a divine gift to Jews, was like a fence around Israel to keep the Hebrews (Israelites, Jews) from mingling with other nations. According to Paul, Torah could not provide righteousness. Paul's understanding is that Torah enclosed all under sin until the coming of the Anointed. Jesus Anointed put an end to the role of Torah, which had been given by God long after he had made a promise to Abraham. Thus, according to Paul, Torah was valid only from its revelation at Mount Sinai (Horeb) to the coming of Christ. Obviously, this temporal limitation of Torah is contrary to Pharisaic Judaism. While Torah plays a limited but positive role in God's redemptive work, it is inferior to the promise God made to Abraham (Gen 17:1–11). Paul's opponents in Galatia

(Jewish-Christians) believed that it provided a way to eternal life; however, Paul taught that life came from the Spirit. Neither life nor righteousness come from Torah (if it did, then the purpose of Jesus Anointed is muted). When the purpose of Torah was completed, Jesus Anointed was sent by God to fulfill the promise made to Abraham and to begin the period of faith, now available to all people: Jews and Gentiles. Because no one is under the Torah, but under faith, there is no reason for either Jews or Gentiles to practice Torah (especially circumcision). Salvation is now available to everyone. Gentiles are sons and daughters of God, adopted through the Spirit. Through baptism, they have been incorporated into the body of Christ; in Pauline understanding, they have put on the Anointed, like one puts on a piece of clothing. Through baptism, they have been transformed, adopted, re-created; they have taken off the old person and put on the new person. What Torah could not do God has accomplished through the Anointed.

Meditation/Journal: What are the implications of Paul's understanding that the time of Torah has passed? Explain.

Psalm Response: "You're blessed when you stay on course, / walking steadily on the road revealed by GOD. / Open my eyes [, GOD,] so I can see / what you show me of your miracle-wonders. / Barricade the road that goes Nowhere; / grace me with your clear revelation. / Give me insight so I can do what you tell me— / my whole life one long, obedient response. / Oh, I'll guard with my life what you've revealed to me, / guard it now, guard it ever . . . . / I meditate on your name all night, GOD, / treasuring your revelation, O GOD." (Ps 119:1, 18, 29, 34, 44, 55, TM)

ABBA

Scripture: ". . . [W]hen the fullness of time had come, God sent his Son, born of a woman, born under the law, in order to redeem those who were under the law, so that we might receive adoption as children. And because you are children, God has sent the Spirit of his Son into our hearts, crying, 'Abba! Father!'" (Gal 4:4–6, NRSVue)

Reflection: At the time fixed by God, according to Paul, he sent his Son (Jesus Anointed) to redeem (buy back) his world. That Son, a human being like all other human beings, was born of a woman, like all other human beings are born. That Jewish boy was born under the time of Torah so that he could redeem all people: Jews and Gentiles. Those under Torah are Jews, who, according to Paul, needed to be set free from trying to earn their salvation by doing the works of Torah. Those not under Torah are Gentiles. No matter whether one was a Jew or a Gentile, God desired to adopt them as his children. Through baptism, one died as a Jew or a Gentile and rose to a new life as a child of God, and as a child of God, each received the Spirit, a gift of God that connects to human spirit in a divine relationship. The Spirit, who takes up residence in the human heart—the core of every human being—urges believers to call God Abba—Aramaic for Father. Because children call their human fathers Abba, God's adopted children—Jews and Gentiles—do the same, prompted by the Spirit. Just like Adam and Eve were the first children of God, Jesus Anointed, Son of God, has restored the relationship of all people with God, since the time of that primordial couple. Thus, just like Jesus Anointed called God his Father, now all Jews and Gentiles do the same, since all of them have been adopted as children of God, according to Paul.

Meditation/Journal: In prayer, how do you address God?

Psalm Response: ". . . [B]less GOD, / From head to toe, I'll bless his holy name! / . . . [B]less GOD, / don't forget a single blessing! / He forgives your sins—every one. / He heals your diseases—every one. / He redeems you . . . —saves your life! / He crowns you with love and mercy—a paradise crown. / He wraps you in goodness—beauty eternal. / He renews your youth—you're always young in his presence. / As parents feel for their children, / GOD feels for those who fear him. / He knows us inside and out, / keeps in mind that we're made of mud." (Ps 103:1–5, 13–14, TM)

CIRCUMCISION (AGAIN)

Scripture: "Listen! I, Paul, am telling you that, if you let yourselves be circumcised, Christ will be of no benefit to you. Once again I testify to every man who lets himself be circumcised that he is obligated to obey the entire law. You who want to be reckoned as righteous by the law have cut yourselves off from Christ; you have fallen away from grace. For through the Spirit, by faith, we eagerly wait for the hope of righteousness. For in Christ Jesus neither circumcision nor uncircumcision counts for anything; the only thing that counts is faith working through love. I wish those who unsettle you would castrate themselves!" (Gal 5:2–6, 12, NRSVue)

Reflection: The Letter to the Galatians is addressed to Gentiles (those who were not Jews, and, therefore, not circumcised). The above passage appears after Paul has declared, "For freedom Christ has set us free" (Gal 5:1a, NRSVue). A Judaizer, a person stating that Gentiles needed to become Jewish first (circumcised) before they could join the movement Paul was preaching, had infiltrated their number and was teaching that all the men needed to be circumcised. While that unsettled no small number of Gentiles, it presented a problem to Pauline theology. According to Paul, circumcision was a work of Torah done to earn salvation; in Paul's thought, righteousness was a free gift offered to both Jews and Gentiles through faith in Anointed Jesus. Any man accepting circumcision, according to Paul, also accepted the entire Torah—all 613 precepts! Thus, circumcision put one back into the yoke of slavery to Torah. Torah could not make people righteous; only God could do that with his grace. Failure to accept grace and trust in Torah (circumcision) cannot bring righteousness. While the Galatian men are considering circumcision, a physical operation, Paul understands it as signifying the acceptance of Judaism. Someone has taught them that it is necessary for salvation, while Paul teaches that they are denying their status as believers in the Anointed and their justification by faith. Acceptance of circumcision for Paul implies the keeping of all Torah, otherwise a single transgression may endanger the whole effort. In Paul's view, the Galatian men are seeking justification by Torah; they have dropped out of grace. They are reneging on the teaching that salvation through the Anointed outside of Torah was sufficient. In other words, they are giving away their freedom. For Paul, salvation is not grounded in Torah (circumcision) but in God's promise to those with faith in the Anointed, and that is the channel of the divine power of love, best illustrated by the Anointed's death on the cross. When one receives the Spirit, one receives divine love's freedom. That is why, according to Paul, neither circumcision (Jews) nor uncircumcision (Gentiles) counts for anything, because it is a work. What counts for righteousness is faith manifested in love of others. It is clear that Paul is exasperated by the Judaizers who advocate circumcision; he adds the sentence that he wishes they would castrate themselves; in other words, he wishes that the knife used for circumcision would slip and turn them into eunuchs!

Meditation/Journal: What modern issue would be the equivalent of the issue of circumcision in Paul's time? In other words, what modern issue deprives believers of their freedom in Christ by advocates insisting that they keep Torah?

Psalm Response: "Don't let those who look to you in hope / Be discouraged by what happens to me, / Dear Lord! . . . / God answer in love! / Answer with your sure salvation! / Now answer me, GOD, because you love me; / Let me see your great mercy full-face. / Don't look the other way; your servant can't take it. / I'm in trouble. Answer right now!" (Ps 69:6a, 13b, 16–17, TM)

SPIRIT VS. FLESH

Scripture: "Live by the Spirit, I say, and do not gratify the desires of the flesh. For what the flesh desires is opposed to the Spirit, and what the Spirit desires is opposed to the flesh, for these are opposed to each other, to prevent you from doing what you want. But if you are led by the Spirit, you are not subject to the law. If we live by the Spirit, let us also be guided by the Spirit. . . . [I]f you sow to the Spirit, you will reap eternal life from the Spirit" (Gal 5:16–18, 25; 6:8, NRSVue)

Reflection: According to Paul, human life is, simply, a way of life. For each person there are different underlying and determining factors that influence human behavior (way of life); the way in which one walks determines the quality of life. While living their way of life, people can live by the Spirit or they can live by the desires of the flesh. Spirit and flesh are opposed to each other. The Spirit is a gift of God which connects the human spirit to the divine Spirit and, ultimately, results in eternal life. The flesh is a force which carries out its own intentions, its own gratifications. In other words, Spirit and flesh are forces acting within each person and waging war against each other; the person is a battlefield. Those who believe in Jesus Anointed are possessed by the Spirit, who leads them; they do not need Torah. They have access to divine life through the Spirit; therefore, that divine life should be manifested in their daily living. Using the metaphors of sowing and reaping (harvesting), Paul concludes that if one sows in the flesh, one harvests what the flesh provides; if one sows in the Spirit, one reaps eternal life.

Meditation/Journal: What aspects of your daily life indicate that you are led by the Spirit? What aspects of your daily life indicate that you are led by the flesh?

Psalm Response: "Listen, GOD! Please, pay attention! / Every morning / you'll hear me at it again. / Every morning / I lay out the pieces of my life . . . . / And here I am, your invited guest— / it's incredible! / I enter your house; here I am, / prostrate in your inner sanctum, / Waiting for directions . . . ." (Ps 5:1, 3, 7–8a, TM)

5

Philippians

THANKSGIVING

Scripture: "I thank my God for every remembrance of you, always in every one of my prayers for all of you, praying with joy for your partnership in the gospel from the first day until now. I am confident of this, that the one who began a good work in you will continue to complete it until the day of Jesus Christ. It is right for me to think this way about all of you, because I hold you in my heart, for all of you are my partners in God's grace, both in my imprisonment and in the defense and confirmation of the gospel." (Phil 1:3–7, NRSVue)

Reflection: The above passage from Paul's Letter to the Philippians contains the longest thanksgiving in any of Paul's letters. In the words above, Paul thanks God for the memories he has of the

Philippians, while he languishes in a Roman prison. His memories of the Philippians, while he is in prison, give him joy, because he remembers the enthusiastic reception of the gospel he preached (Jesus Anointed died, was buried, and was raised) and that they became partners in the gospel with him. His memories of partnership in his mission give him comfort; in other words, from Paul's perspective the Philippians are a success story; from the first day of Paul's preaching until the writing of the letter, they have been constant. This gives him confidence that they will remain instruments of God's work (Phil 2:13) until the day of Jesus Anointed (Parousia, Christ's return in glory). The Philippians' reliability affects Paul emotionally; at his core, he holds them in his heart. All of them and he share God's grace, no matter that he is in prison and they are not. Their partnership with him in the gospel is personal. Paul's feelings for the Philippians are stirred by his fond memories of them.

Meditation/Journal: Which of your memories bring you comfort, joy, and grace?

Psalm Response: "I'm thanking you, GOD, from a full heart, / I'm writing the book on your wonders. / I'm whistling, laughing, and jumping for joy; / I'm singing your song, High God. / You took over and set everything right; / when I needed you, you were there, taking charge. / GOD holds the high center, / he sees and sets the world's mess right. / He decides what is right for us earthlings, / gives people their just des[s]erts." (Ps 9:1-2, 4, 7-8, TM)

PROGRESS

Scripture: "I want you to know . . . that what has happened to me has actually resulted in the progress of the gospel, so that it has become known throughout the whole imperial guard and to everyone else that my imprisonment is for Christ . . . . I know that through your prayers and the help of the Spirit of Jesus Christ this will turn out for my salvation. For to me, living is Christ and dying is gain. If I am to live in the flesh that means fruitful labor for me, yet I cannot say which I will choose. I am hard pressed between the two; my desire is to depart and be with Christ, for that is far better, but to remain in the flesh is more necessary for you." (Phil 1:12–13, 19, 21–24, NRSVue)

Reflection: According to Paul, his imprisonment has not only failed to hinder the spread of the gospel, but, on the contrary, it has aided its progress. Thus, he rejoices (Phil 1:18). Those outside his immediate circle have heard about his imprisonment for the Anointed, even the Imperial Guard in Rome; the Imperial Guard was responsible for political prisoners. Paul is addressing how the Philippians should think about his situation, and he is telling them that they should view his imprisonment as, paradoxically, gospel-progress. Because Paul's imprisonment has resulted in the progress of the gospel, he is confident that it will lead to his salvation. Thus, the Philippians' prayers and the indwelling Spirit of the Anointed will be for the good of both Paul and the gospel he preaches. He expects to continue to live in the Anointed, even though he believes that death will bring him into the presence of the Anointed. As he tells the Philippians, continuing to live in the flesh means that he will have to continue to preach the gospel. While he seems to be caught between a rock and hard place, he has already decided to pursue life in the flesh for the good of the Philippians. He is worried that they are not making progress in the gospel, and his presence will reverse that trend. From an altruistic point of view, he will delay his possible death—as the result of imprisonment—for their sakes, even though his first choice is to die and be with the Anointed.

Meditation/Journal: What experience have you had that first looked like imminent defeat but turned out to be victory? Explain.

Psalm Response: "GOD answer you on the day you crash, / The name God . . . put you out of harm's reach, / Send reinforcements . . . , / Dispatch . . . fresh supplies, / Exclaim over you . . . , / Celebrate . . . , / Give you what your heart desires, / Accomplish your plans. / When you win, we plan to raise the roof / and lead the parade with our banners. / May all your wishes come true! / That clinches it—help's coming, / an answer's on the way, / everything's going to work out." (Ps 20:1–6, TM)

CONFIDENCE

Scripture: "If anyone . . . has reason to be confident in the flesh, I have more: circumcised on the eighth day, a member of the people of Israel, of the tribe of Benjamin, a Hebrew born of Hebrews; as to the law, a Pharisee; as to zeal, a persecutor of the church; as to righteousness under the law, blameless. Yet whatever gains I had, these I have come to regard as loss because of Christ. More than that, I regard everything as loss because of the surpassing value of knowing Christ Jesus my Lord. For his sake I have suffered the loss of all things, and I regard them as rubbish, in order that I may gain Christ and be found in him, not having a righteousness of my own that comes from the law but one that comes through faith in Christ, the righteousness from God based on faith. I want to know Christ and the power of his resurrection . . . ." (Phil 3:4b–10, NRSVue)

Reflection: After telling the Philippians to "rejoice in the Lord" (Phil 3:1), Paul notes that there are two basic ways to relate to God: boasting in Christ or putting confidence in the flesh. Then, he presents why earlier life gave him reason to be confident in the flesh: circumcision, being an Israelite of the tribe of Benjamin from whom his namesake—King Saul—came, having Hebrew parents, a Torah-abiding Pharisee, a persecutor of Anointed's followers; and blamelessly righteous according to Torah. Those former identity markers are contrasted to the ones he has chosen as an Anointed believer with a desire to know Anointed Jesus. Indeed, in light of his new identity markers, everything in the past is loss, rubbish, garbage when compared to the gain of knowing Anointed Jesus. In his Second Letter to the Corinthians, he wrote about "the light of the knowledge of the glory of God in the face of Christ" (2 Cor 4:6, NRSVue). Earlier in his Second Letter to the Corinthians, he had stated that "what once had glory has . . . lost its glory because of the greater glory" (2 Cor 3:10) of knowing Anointed Jesus. In other words, what once was important is no longer important because Paul has been transformed through faith in the Anointed, from which comes righteousness. Further transformation awaits, as Paul wants also to share in the power of the Anointed's resurrection (salvation).

Meditation/Journal: In your life experience, what did you once consider gain that you now consider loss? Explain. What transformation occurred in you? In your life experience what did you once consider loss that you now consider gain? Explain. What transformation occurred in you?

Psalm Response: "Thank GOD because he's good, / because his love never quits. / Tell the world, / 'His love never quits.' / Far better to take refuge in GOD / than trust in people; / Far better to take refuge in GOD / than trust in celebrities. / GOD's my strength, he's also my song, / and now he's my salvation. / I didn't die. I *lived*! / And now I'm telling the world what GOD did." (Ps 118:1, 8–9, 14, 17, TM)

CITIZENSHIP

Scripture: ". . . [O]ur citizenship is in heaven, and it is from there that we are expecting a Savior, the Lord Jesus Christ. He will transform the body of our humiliation that it may be conformed to the body of his glory, by the power that also enables him to make all things subject to himself." (Phil 3:20–21, NRSVue)

Reflection: Citizenship in Paul's world, as well as our own, was the legal status of being a citizen of a country, into which one was born or legally accepted. In his Letter to the Philippians, Paul applies that legal idea to the gospel he preaches. He reminds the Philippians that both he and they are citizens of the heavens, the area above the dome of the sky where God lived. The reader must keep in mind that biblical people lived in a three-storied universe; a good picture of that universe is a three-storied skyscraper! On the first floor, named the underworld or Sheol, is where the dead lived; on the second floor, the earth, is where people lived; and above the dome that covered the earth, the heavens, is where God lived. From the heavens, citizens of heaven living on the earth, were expecting the return of the Anointed (Jesus Messiah, Christ). Paul believed that he would be alive when this event took place. "The

Lord is near," he writes (Phil 4:5b, NRSVue). In his First Letter to the Thessalonians, he writes that they "wait for [God's] Son from heaven" (1 Thess 1:10, NRSVue). Paul's basic idea is that final salvation will be a metamorphosis, a change of form. Those believers in the Anointed have already been conformed to the Anointed's death in this life on earth through baptism. When the Anointed returns, they will have their bodies transformed, so that they are conformed to the glorious body of the Anointed. According to the hymn he quotes in chapter 2 of the Letter to Philippians, it is God who exalted the Anointed (Phil 2:9–11); however, in 3:21, it is the Anointed's own power that will be the agent of transformation.

Meditation/Journal: Of what (country, nation, land, kingdom, group, etc.) are you a citizen? Explain.

Psalm Response: "GOD sovereignly brought me to my knees, / he cut me down in my prime. / 'Oh, don't,' I prayed, 'please don't let me die. / You have more years than you know what to do with! / You laid earth's foundations a long time ago, / and handcrafted the very heavens; / You'll still be around when they're long gone, / threadbare and discarded like an old suit of clothes. / You'll throw them away like a worn-out coat, / but year after year you're as good as new. / Your servants' children will have a good place to live / and their children will be at home with you.'" (Ps 102:23–28, TM)

6

First Thessalonians

CHOSEN

Scripture: ". . . [W]e know, . . . beloved by God, that he has chosen you, because our message of the gospel came to you not in word only but also in power and in the Holy Spirit and with full conviction . . . . For the word of the Lord has sounded forth from you . . . in every place your faith in God has become known, so that we have no need to speak about it. . . . [A]nd to wait for [God's] Son from heaven, whom he raised from the dead—Jesus . . . ." (1 Thess 1:4–5, 8, 10, NRSVue)

Reflection: Paul is thankful to God for the Thessalonians, who have been chosen by God to receive the gospel (the Anointed died, was buried, and was raised by God). It was not only the preaching of the gospel—the word—but also the power, its divine source, and the connection of the Holy Spirit to the spirits of the Thessalonians, both individually and collectively, that made them a model community, according to Paul. Like a megaphone, the word of God has emanated from them, so that their fame as believers has spread everywhere. Now, they, according to one of Paul's beliefs, await the coming of the dead, buried, and raised Anointed.

Meditation/Journal: What word of God echoes from you? Be specific.

Psalm Response: "[Madam Day and Professor Night's] words aren't heard, / their voices aren't recorded, / But their silence fills the earth, / unspoken truth is spoken everywhere. / . . . God's Word vaults across the skies / from sunrise to sunset, / Melting ice, scorching deserts, / warming hearts to faith. / The revelation of GOD is whole / and pulls our lives together." (Ps 19:3–4, 6–7, TM)

WORD

Scripture: "We also constantly give thanks to God for this, that when you received the word of God that you heard from us you accepted it not as a human word but as what it really is, God's word, which is also at work in you believers." (1 Thess 2:13, NRSVue)

Reflection: In Pauline understanding, faith is a gift whose human response is gratitude to God. In the above passage from Paul's First Letter to the Thessalonians—often considered a collection of letters edited to look like a single letter—the author thanks God for the Thessalonians' reception of the message he preached. Their discernment that Paul's words were gospel words emphasizes the message and its acceptance not as human word, but as divine word. In other words, the Thessalonians concluded that Paul was delivering God's word to them, while the same God was at work in their lives. This means that the real reason for the success of Paul's mission was God's active part in it. Thus, the Thessalonians recognized the divine word that Paul delivered because the author of that divine word was already at work—usually through the Spirit—in the lives of those Thessalonians who accepted it as divine word.

Meditation/Journal: If you critique Paul's words about God being at work in the lives of the Thessalonians who accepted his preaching as divine word of God, what do you discover? In your lifetime, whose words have you received as God's word? Explain.

Prayer Response: "May God our Father himself and our Master Jesus clear the road to you! And may the Master pour on the love so it fills your lives and splashes over on everyone around you, just as it does from us to you. May you be infused with strength and purity, filled with confidence in the presence of God our Father when our Master Jesus arrives with all his followers." (1 Thess 3:11–13, TM)

DEAD

Scripture: ". . . [W]e do not want you to be uninformed . . . about those who have died, so that you may not grieve as others do who have no hope. For since we believe that Jesus died and rose again, even so, through Jesus, God will bring with him those who have died. For this we declare to you by the word of the Lord, that we who are alive, who are left until the coming of the Lord, will by no means precede those who have died. For the Lord himself with a cry of command, with the archangel's call and with the sound of God's trumpet, will descend from heaven, and the dead in Christ will rise first. Then we who are alive, who are left, will be caught up in the clouds together with them to meet the Lord in the air, and so we will be with the Lord forever. (1 Thess 4:13–17, NRSVue)

Reflection: Paul's scenario about what will happen when Jesus Anointed returns (Parousia) is based on his world's conception that the universe was, basically, a three-floored skyscraper. From the bottom up, the first floor was where the dead lived (Sheol); the middle floor was where people lived (earth); and the top floor was where God and Jesus Anointed lived (heaven). The Thessalonians have sent Paul a question: What will happen to those who have died (first floor) when Jesus Anointed returns from the top floor to the middle floor? Because he wants his readers to be fully informed and not sink into despair, like some other people who have no hope, Paul appeals to the basic gospel he preaches: Jesus died, was buried, and God raised the Anointed from the dead. That belief should give hope to the Thessalonians. As he gets ready to narrate the event of the Parousia, he reminds his readers that he speaks with a prophetic voice. God's call is not negated by death; the living have no advantage over the dead, even though some living believers are essential for welcoming the Anointed when he returns! There will be pomp and circumstance when the Anointed descends from the top floor to the middle floor. Those on the first floor—the dead in Christ—are those who belonged to the Anointed, hoped in him, and died committed to him. At his divine command, they will be raised from the first floor to the second floor; this will take place as an angelic voice announces that the Anointed has arrived to gather the elect and awaken the dead to life. God's trumpet, a sign of the theophany taking place, will sound to notify everyone of the approach of the Anointed. According to Paul, once the dead have been raised from the first floor to the second floor, those on the second floor will be caught up in the clouds—another sign of a theophany—so that all—formerly dead and living—are united to meet the Anointed while rising in the air from the second floor to the top floor. Then, the goal of the commitment of the formerly dead and the living to Jesus Anointed will be achieved; they will live with the Anointed forever. Thus, the Thessalonians have their question answered; now, they are informed about those who have died!

Meditation/Journal: In light of the modern cosmological understanding of the earth as being one planet among others rotating around the sun, what happens to Paul's three-storied universe description of Jesus Anointed's return? Using modern cosmological understanding, how would you describe Jesus Anointed's return?

Prayer Response: "May God himself, the God who makes everything holy and whole, make you holy and whole, put you together—spirit, soul, and body—and keep you fit for the coming of our Master, Jesus Christ. The One who called you is completely dependable. If he said it, he'll do it!" (1 Thess 5:23–24, TM)

TIMES AND SEASONS

Scripture: "Now concerning the times and the seasons, . . . you do not need to have anything written to you. For you yourselves know very well that the day of the Lord will come like a thief in the night. . . . [Y]ou . . . are not in darkness, for that day to surprise you like a thief; for you are all children of light and children of the day; we are not of the night or of darkness. So, then, let us not fall asleep as others do, but let us keep awake and be sober, for those who sleep sleep at night, and those who are drunk get drunk at night. But since we belong to the day, let us be sober and put on the breastplate of faith and love and for a helmet the hope of salvation. For God has destined us . . . for obtaining salvation through our Lord Jesus Christ, who died for us, so that whether we are awake or asleep we may live with him." (1 Thess 5:1–2, 4–10, NRSVue)

Reflection: In the Thessalonian community, the return of the Anointed (Parousia) was an important topic. In a question to Paul, they want to know when it will occur. Of course, Paul cannot answer their question; indeed, over two thousand years later the question still cannot be answered—nor has it occurred! The Anointed's (Lord's) day is borrowed from the prophet Amos (5:18–20) and the prophet Joel (2:32), and it was used to refer to Jesus' return in glory. A common comparison was the day would come unexpectedly, like a thief in the night, an image used many times in the Christian Bible (New Testament) (Matt 24:23–24; Luke 12:39–40; Rev 3:3, 16:15; 2 Pet 3:10). Paul reminds his readers that they are not in darkness; thus, the day will not surprise them. Using dualistic imagery, he tells them that they are children of light and day; while the Lord's day will still come upon them unexpectedly, it will not be like a thief at night. In other words, Paul tells the Thessalonians that they are prepared for anytime and any season. For Paul, night and day illustrate the inevitability of the Parousia, while darkness and light illustrate the daily struggle to remain committed in faith to the Anointed. Because no one knows (if or) when the day of the Lord will occur, Paul exhorts his readers to vigilance, awareness, self-control, and balance (staying awake);

he wants them to be motivated by the coming of the Lord's day. Their readiness is like putting on armor: the breastplate is faith and love, and the helmet is the hope of salvation, to which God has destined all who believe that Jesus Anointed died, was buried, and was raised. It makes no difference if believers are alive or dead, their hope is to live with him (be saved).

Meditation/Journal: What do you understand the day of the Lord to be? Explain. What metaphor—other than "like a thief in the night"—could you use for the day of the Lord? Explain.

Psalm Response: "Get insurance with GOD and do a good deed, / settle down and stick to your last. / Keep company with GOD, get in on the best. / Open up before GOD, keep nothing back; / he'll do whatever needs to be done: / He'll validate your life in the clear light of day / and stamp you with approval at high noon. / Quiet down before GOD, / be prayerful before him." (Ps 37:3–7a, TM)

7

Philemon

ONESIMUS

Scripture: ". . . To our beloved coworker Philemon, . . . and to the church in your house; Grace to you and peace from God our Father and the Lord Jesus Christ. . . . I . . . appeal to you on the basis of love—and I, Paul, do this as an old man and now also as a prisoner of Christ Jesus. I am appealing to you for my child, Onesimus, whose father I have become during my imprisonment. Formerly he was useless to you, but now he is indeed useful to you and to me. I am sending him, that is, my own heart, back to you. I wanted to keep him with me so that he might minister to me in your place during my imprisonment for the gospel, but I preferred to do nothing without your consent in order that your good deed might be voluntary and not something forced. . . . [S]o that you

might have him back . . . no longer as a slave but more than a slave,
a beloved brother . . . . So if you consider me your partner, welcome him as you would welcome me. Refresh my heart in Christ.
(Phlm 1:1b, 2–3, 9–14, 16–17, 20b, NRSVue)

Reflection: While Paul's Letter to Philemon looks like a letter to
a private individual—Philemon—it is, in fact, a letter to the community whose members meet in his house. Philemon was rich
enough to own a home large enough to provide a place for a group
of people to meet. At some point in time he had met Paul, who
facilitated his coming to faith in Jesus Anointed. Furthermore, he
owns at least one slave—Onesimus—who ran away, found Paul,
and ministered to him. While that was taking place, he, too, came
to believe in Jesus Anointed. So, the time has come for Paul to
obey the civil law and return Philemon's runaway slave along with
the Letter to Philemon, only twenty-five verses long. The letter
intercedes for Onesimus in the hope that love will be promoted
by beloved Philemon's decision and deed. As a member of a community showing mutual love, Paul urges Philemon to manifest
that love in accepting Onesimus. Philemon's decision will affect
the whole community that gathers in his house (Phlm 1:2). If faith
working through love is present in Philemon, then he, a well-to-do
man, will, according to Paul, accept Onesimus as a brother—not as
a slave! In Philemon's and Paul's world, a runaway slave could be
pursued by his owner taking out a warrant against him; if he were
apprehended, he had to be returned to his master, who could pun-
ish him as he willed. Paul is asking Philemon to ignore his rights
as a slave owner and to do his duty as a fellow believer. Paul refers
to Onesimus as his child, for whom, like a father, he is interceding.
This makes Philemon brother to Onesimus! And there is more:
While Onesimus was useless to Philemon because of his runaway
status, he is now useful—the meaning of his name, Onesimus.
Furthermore, the Greek words for useless and useful allude to the
Greek word for Anointed, Christos. In other words, according to
Paul, Onesimus has been transformed into a member of the body
of Christ, the community that meets in Philemon's house and is
now a brother in Christ to all the members of that community.

Paul urges Philemon in love to make his decision about Onesimus, as the master-slave relationship has been surpassed by love in Jesus Anointed.

Meditation/Journal: If you were Philemon, what would you do with the returned slave Onesimus? Explain. What experience have you had that undoes the master-slave relationship and replaces it with the human-human love relationship? Explain.

Psalm Response: "God's love is meteoric, / his loyalty astronomic, / His purpose titanic, / his verdicts oceanic. / Yet in his largeness / nothing gets lost; / How exquisite your love, O God! / How eager we are to run under your wings, / To eat our fill at the banquet you spread / as you fill our tankards with Eden spring water. / You're a fountain of cascading light, / and you open our eyes to light. / Keep on loving your friends; / do your work in welcoming hearts." (Ps 37:5–6a, 7–10, TM)

St. Romans

P 1 Corinthians

2 Corinthians

A Galatians

U Philippians

l 1 Thessalonians

Philemon

Concluding Summary

BECAUSE PAUL IS A Jewish Pharisee trained in Torah, he believes that God is in charge of everything. Whatever happens in the world does so because either God wills it or permits it to happen. While the earliest of Paul's letters is First Thessalonians, in general Pauline letters are arranged in the Bible according to length. All Paul's letters are written earlier than gospels (Mark, Matthew, Luke, John), so when Paul uses the word *gospel*, he is not referring to one of the four canonical gospels but to his good news (creed): Anointed Jesus was crucified, died, buried, and raised from the dead by God. Thus, Paul's letters contain what biblical scholars have determined to be one of many forms of what is today called early Christianity. In other words, Pauline Christianity was one of several that developed in the known world in the early centuries CE.

Paul considered himself to be a servant (slave) of Jesus Anointed. He called himself an apostle, sent primarily to the Gentiles (non-Jews), most likely Gentile sympathizers often called God-fearers. He called himself the least of apostles, because before he was overwhelmed by grace and set apart to preach the good news of Jesus Anointed's death, burial, and resurrection he persecuted the very group he later joined! He considered himself a recipient of divine revelation concerning Jesus Anointed, a Jewish descendant, raised from the dead by the Spirit as a demonstration of God's love for people.

In his letters, Paul interprets the event of Anointed Jesus' death, burial, and resurrection and what it meant for those Gentiles to whom he preached and wrote follow-up letters to the small communities of believers he founded. Basically, Paul though that God re-created the world through Jesus Anointed. Through Jesus Anointed, God justified people with grace. People, who inherited the sin of Adam, were acquitted of sin or made right in their relationship with God; all they needed to do was to respond to God's offer with faith in Jesus Anointed—dead, buried, and raised by God—to receive and accept God's righteousness. In other words, God's righteousness was definitely revealed in Paul's gospel to both Jews and Gentiles without any further practices of Torah.

Grace, a free gift of God's own self to people, cannot be earned. If one can justify oneself by keeping all 613 precepts of Torah, then what is the meaning of the Jesus Anointed event? Jesus Anointed is himself an example of justification by grace through faith. As a human being, he accepted God's free gift and lived according to it. He was the person in whom God was at work reconciling the world to himself. He was the person whose faith remained through death and resurrection. He was the person God called and through whom God saved or rescued the world. He was the person whom people believe God raised from the dead. He was the person who demonstrated God's love and his reliability. He was a new Adam. God rescued (saved) people and delivered them from their alienation from God, caused by Adam, through their faith in Jesus' resurrection. The revelation of God was obedience to faith, not obedience to Torah.

For Paul, sin was the attempt by people to earn salvation or righteousness by obedience to Torah; by keeping all 613 precepts of Torah (Law), Pharisaic Judaism thought people could earn salvation. Paul refers to that practice as disobedience; it is the person's attempt to establish his or her own justification or righteousness.

Obedience, for Paul, is the acceptance of God's free gift with a demonstratable response, known as behavior or lifestyle. People are not saved because of their behavior; they are saved because they accept God's gift and, through the way they live, demonstrate their acceptance of the divine gift.

This means that people are free from attempting to earn salvation. Reconciliation between God and people has been accomplished by God through Jesus Anointed. All those who believe that God reconciled the world to himself in Jesus Anointed participate in baptism into his death and resurrection. After they—looking like Adam—die with the Anointed in baptism, they are raised to new life and become members of the community, the body of Christ; each individual in the community has been given gifts by the Spirit (who raised Jesus) for the common good of the whole community. For Paul, spirituality is the Spirit-spirit connection. The divine Spirit is connected to each individual spirit; thus, each person's spiritual gift is for the good of the spirituality of the whole community. Furthermore, no one can boast of his or her gift, because it is God's doing, God's mercy manifested.

In order to illustrate this, Paul constructs the old Adam-new Adam comparison. The old Adam represents all the people from Adam to Jesus who inherited Adam's disobedience (attempt to be God) with the result of death. God had made the offer of grace to the old Adam, but he refused and messed up everything for all who followed him. Jesus, the new Adam, obeyed God; he, God's Son, didn't even attempt to be God, but became a servant of God; because of his obedience, he straightened out everything for everyone. The old Adam brought death; the new Adam (Anointed Jesus) brought life. Through baptism, people participate in Jesus Anointed's death and resurrection; they become sons and daughters of God. Then, they live their lives as demonstrated by the new Adam, Jesus Anointed.

According to Paul, through, in, and by the Anointed, God has declared all people justified. God has re-offered righteousness (a relationship with God). God has redeemed (repurchased) people. God has reconciled (undone the separation caused by

Adam) through Jesus Anointed. This means that now people have undeserved honor, holiness (sanctification), freedom (no need to earn salvation through Torah); estrangement has been removed (atonement). People now can share in the victory over Adam's sin as they wait for the new Adam, Jesus, to return. Paul thought that Jesus' return was imminent, and that he would still be around to witness it.

The God who is in charge of everything has rescued (saved) people through Jesus Anointed. In other words, God has re-created through Jesus, his human instrument. Paul interprets this to mean that both Jews and Gentiles can be saved. Salvation is for all, even Jews who do not believe. God has a plan, according to Paul; sometimes he hardens hearts for a reason, while at other times he shows mercy. In other words, in the past God chosen Abram (Abraham) to be the father of many nations (Jews and Gentiles), and God justified Abraham through his faith (trust). God offered him grace, and he responded with faith which justified him or made him righteous. He lived according to his faith (trust) in God without Torah. After Moses, one of Abraham's descendants, was called by God to lead the Hebrews out of Egyptian slavery, God gave his chosen people the Torah, which, according to Paul, was God's way of exposing sin. However, instead of being a way of life, Torah became a way of self-justification. Paul says that the time for Torah passed away with the arrival of Jesus Anointed.

In Pauline thought, it is not that works are not important. It is simply that the works of Torah (circumcision is the big one) are not done to attempt to earn salvation. Works are done in response to the acceptance of God's offer of salvation (righteousness).

Jesus Anointed, Lord and Son of God through resurrection by the power of the Spirit, obeyed God, trusted God, and became a model of faithfulness—not to mention that he revealed who God is and what God does. God chose (Anointed) Jesus and worked through him to bring redemption, salvation, reconciliation, atonement, and peace to Jews and Gentiles. God validated this starting over by raising the dead and buried Jesus. While waiting for the Anointed's return, Paul preached to both Jews (attempting to earn righteousness by keeping Torah) and Gentiles (who had never heard of Torah) about Jesus' death, burial, and resurrection. From the time of Jesus through the time of the body of Christ, while awaiting the Anointed's return, Adamic people die to Torah in baptism and rise looking like Christ. They live new life in the Anointed animated by the Spirit; they are children of God now, Spirit-filled and saved, calling God "Abba, Father."

Paul refers to himself as the apostle to the Gentiles. Because of his perspective that God was doing something new in Jesus Anointed, Paul states that the time of Torah has passed. God's chosen people now includes both Jews and Gentiles. Some Jews and some Jews believing in Jesus Anointed think that before Gentiles can be admitted—to what we today call Christianity—they must become Jews first. For men, this implies circumcision, the sign of the covenant God entered with Abraham. Paul understands circumcision as a work of Torah and, as such, as an attempt to earn salvation. Thus, Paul sees no reason to practice it; Gentile men are more than happy not to observe it! In Paul's understanding, it means nothing anymore. This, of course, upsets both Torah-observing Jews and Jewish-Christians, who used to observe Torah. Paul, who was himself circumcised on the eighth day after his birth, declares that in light of what God did in Jesus Anointed circumcision or lack of it means nothing. What means something is *agape*, self-sacrificing love in the community; *agape* fulfills Torah.

According to Paul, God had been covenanting with people and making them righteous outside of Torah. Jesus Anointed represents another divine move both to Jews and Gentiles. Because people cannot approach God until God approaches them, he has revealed himself in the person of Jesus Anointed and offered them righteousness and given them the grace to respond in freedom to his offer. It is important to note that in Pauline thought people do not have absolute freedom; they have the freedom God gives them. There is free will, but there is very little of it! Because faith is a way of life, a lifestyle of love, Paul cannot imagine anyone not living in relationship with God and using Jesus Anointed as his or her model. Paul does not tell Jews or Gentiles to believe in Jesus; he tells them to believe in God and do what Jesus did, live in relationship with God. There is no need for Torah observance. Anyone in a relationship with God will always do the right thing because it is the right thing to do, while waiting for the day of the Lord Jesus' return in glory.

Bibliography

Crossan, John Dominic. *Paul the Pharisee: A Vision Beyond the Violence of Civilization*. Salem, OR: Polebridge, 2024.

New Revised Standard Version Updated Edition, Apocryphal/Deuterocanonical Books of the Old Testament. Grand Rapids, MI: Zondervan, 2022.

O'Day, Gail R, and David Peterson. *The Access Bible: New Revised Standard Version with the Apocryphal/Deuterocanonical Books*. New York: Oxford University Press, 1999.

Peterson, Eugene, and William Griffin. *The Message: Catholic/Ecumenical Edition, The Bible in Contemporary Language*. Chicago: ACTA, 2013.

Recent Books by Mark G. Boyer
Published by Wipf & Stock

Nature Spirituality: Praying with Wind, Water, Earth, Fire

A Spirituality of Ageing

Weekday Saints: Reflections on Their Scriptures

Human Wholeness: A Spirituality of Relationship

A Simple Systematic Mariology

Praying Your Way through Luke's Gospel and the Acts of the Apostles

An Abecedarian of Animal Spirit Guides: Spiritual Growth through Reflections on Creatures

Overcome with Paschal Joy: Chanting through Lent and Easter— Daily Reflections with Familiar Hymns

Taking Leave of Your Home: Moving in the Peace of Christ

An Abecedarian of Sacred Trees: Spiritual Growth through Reflections on Woody Plants

Divine Presence: Elements of Biblical Theophanies

Fruit of the Vine: A Biblical Spirituality of Wine

Names for Jesus: Reflections for Advent and Christmas

Talk to God and Listen to the Casual Reply: Experiencing the Spirituality of John Denver

www.ingramcontent.com/pod-product-compliance
Lightning Source LLC
Chambersburg PA
CBHW071835090426
42737CB00012B/2248